MW01168845

Garland

Garland

The History of the Gate City
as Told by the Residents

By Christy Fleming

Copyright 2008 by Christy Fleming

All rights reserved.
No part of this book may be reproduced by any means,
electronic or mechanical, including photocopying, without written permission.

Book and cover design by K.T. Roes.

Published by WordsWorth
1285 Sheridan Avenue, No. 275
Cody, Wyoming   82414

ISBN 0-9771286-4-4

This book is dedicated to the residents of Garland, Wyoming,
past, present and future.

Susan,
Thank you for your help!
Hope you enjoy! Lots of
Love
Christy *[signature]*

Contents

Author's Notes

First of all, I would like to thank everyone who gave me information, photos, and interviews. I had a wonderful time connecting with all of you. I was graciously invited into people's homes, was fed, and even sung to, on one occasion. It was a great experience. Without the openness, honesty, and the sharing attitude of every person who shared, this book would not have been possible. I am only sorry that some of these wonderful people have passed on before the project was completed.

I also have to thank my family and friends. Without their encouragement, and sometimes nagging, I would probably have never completed the book. They all know who they are, and I am grateful to all of them. A big "Thank You" also goes out to Carole Randall for doing the editing.

I grew up in the Garland area and had heard stories about the Honey Hill Farm and the store in Garland, but never anything about other businesses and goings on. One day, I was talking with my brother-in-law Mike Fleming and his friend Nick Frank and they started talking about Garland's early years and its hotels, saloons, and houses of ill repute. This fascinated me, and a couple of years later I decided to gather the information about Garland and put it into a book.

Some earlier residents had written essays and garnered information about Garland, but I quickly realized that there was much more that could be written down. I wanted to collect the stories before they were lost forever, so I began to interview people who still live in or had once lived in Garland.

With time, details and events have become foggy, and, as any historian will tell you, no two people usually see or remember the same event in the same way. That was one of the most interesting parts of gathering material for this book. People, without knowing it, filled in the gaps of each other's stories.

There are still gaps. This is, by no means, the complete history of Garland. There are still stories out there that could be added, but this is what I found during my seven years of interviews, research, and writing. All of it has been compiled for posterity. The photos, interviews, newspaper clippings, and anything else that was gathered during the writing of this book have been donated to the Homesteader Museum in Powell, Wyoming.

I hope that you enjoy this book about the people who have lived in the little community of Garland, Wyoming. This is their story.

Christy Fleming
Garland, Wyoming
April, 2008

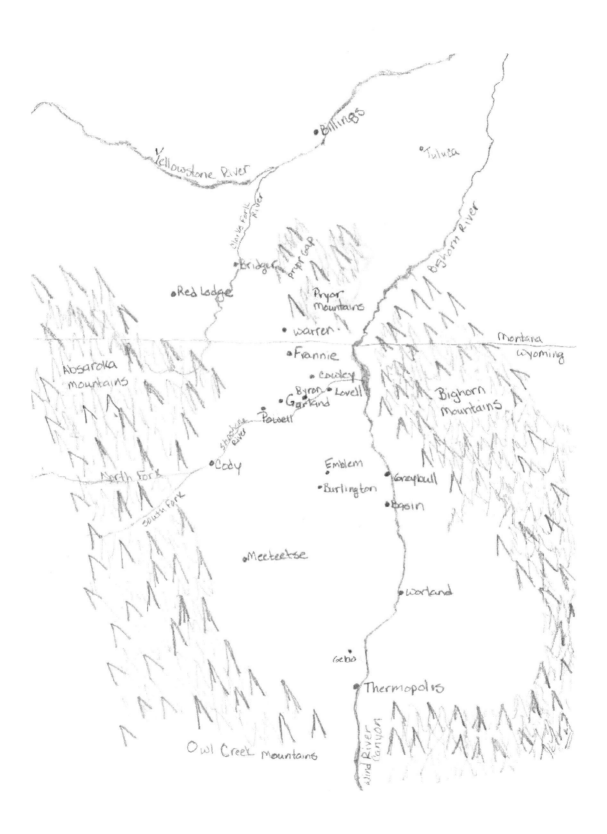

Chapter 1 - How It All Began

Driving through Garland today, most people would find it difficult to imagine it as a bustling town with hotels, bars, restaurants, clothing and grocery stores, and a hardware store. All that remains today are a few homes, clumped along the highway, and the ASI Bean Mill. People pass through Garland every day and probably wonder why they have to slow down to 45 m.p.h. It most likely never crosses their minds, as they make the curve on their way west to Powell, Wyoming, that the few remaining homes are vestiges of what was once a thriving community.

However, they might see the sign: "Garland: population – 50." This sign and the big, white church are the only clues that this little community was ever any larger. Garland was never incorporated, but evidence from the January 13, 1906, issue of the local newspaper shows that efforts were made in that direction. *The Garland Guard* asked, "Can anyone tort out a reasonable excuse why Garland should not be incorporated? If so, tort it out." Unfortunately, someone must have taken this challenge seriously, as an incorporation failed to occur. Still, Garland, without the benefit of this legal action, became home to a growing population that experienced the joys and problems of any western town. In its time, Garland was the place to be.

So how did it all begin? There doesn't seem to be a defining moment, but the availability of water, with Bitter Creek and the Shoshone River nearby, seems to have drawn people. As early as 1864, Jim Bridger was leading a party of 300 people, with 62 wagons, from Denver to the gold fields of Montana. To avoid the Indian troubles on the Bozeman Trail, Bridger chose an alternate route through the Bighorn Basin. It was not as dangerous but had less available water. It makes sense though that Bridger, an experienced mountain man, brought travelers through this area and took advantage of the water resources. Evidence of this truth comes to us from *Wyoming's Bighorn Basin to 1901*:

> "Another dry march north brought them to the Stinking Water near the present site of Garland. The party then rested to await the arrival of two additional trains following from the south. All three trains were together on June 18th." (B12)

Although the Bridger Trail never really caught on, Ted Lord, a long-time Garland resident, said that by 1885, a freight road was coming through Garland. The freighters came from Red Lodge or Billings into Garland. From there, the road continued to Penrose, across Whistle Creek and Coon Creeks, following closely the present Emblem to Powell highway. Then it forded Dry Creek and came up on the bench straight north of the Emblem schoolhouse and southeast over Table Mountain. (B4)

Vying with Cody for trade, Garland became the freighting center for the Bighorn Basin. (NA6) Its freight came from the railheads in Billings and Red Lodge, Montana. Freight teams mostly consisted of horses or mules, though oxen were sometimes used instead. A small team was composed of a freighter (possibly a farmer or rancher trying to supplement his income) and four to eight horses pulling one wagon. A larger team could pull two wagons. (B9) Large freight teams hauled goods from Garland to Lovell, Byron, Basin, Shell, Hyattville, Emblem, Burlington, Worland, and even as far away as Thermopolis. On their return trip, they brought wool, honey, and other goods to be shipped back to the railheads. (NA7)

In the late summer of 1901, after the Burlington and Missouri River Railroad arrived in Garland, Samuel T. Johnson and John A. Garfield, of Burlington, made improvements to the freight road from Garland to Germania (present-day Emblem). They placed sticks along the route to mark the path for the team and walking plow to follow. The team plowed a furrow, creating the road to Germania and Burlington, Otto, and Basin. (B9) The Bighorn County map of this area, for the years of 1901 to 1905, shows stagelines used at the time. The stage lines went from Garland to Byron to Cowley, then to Lovell, down to Iona, ending at Kane. The major line, probably following the freight route, left the Garland line going to Germania, Otto, Basin, and Jordan - which was a dividing point. From Jordan, one line followed the No Wood River to Bonanza, Hyattville, Ten Sleep, and Cedar, ending at Big Trails. The other stageline went to Thermopolis. (B9)

Norman "Pete" Woods remembered the freight wagons and horses coming across his dad's homestead. His family had fenced everything that had been open range, including part of the freighters' road. The freighters, who were accustomed to going their own way without having to go around the homesteaders' fences, just cut through anything that impeded them and kept going. (I27)

(Parts of that old freight road can still be seen today, thanks to Bonnie Hiller's father, Walter Brown. The freight lines were still running when her father was homesteading. He planted silver leaf poplars on each side of the freight line, as it came by their homestead. Some of those trees are still there, though others were cut down as they grew old and dangerous.) (I15) According to Lucy Cozzens, on the way back to Red Lodge, there was a steep hill her husband, Fred, had shown her one day while they were out in the hills. He told her that the freighters had tied up to a big tree on the top of the hill and slowly allowed the horses to draw the wagons and goods down. The freighters did this so that

Walter Brown planted these silver leaf poplars on each side of the freight road that can still be seen today.

the wagon would not get out of control as it went down the steep hill. If it got away, it could run over the horses and upset the wagon, sending goods and supplies to the bottom. Lucy recalls that at the base of the hill, there was a lot of rotting wood, so apparently this technique did not always work. (I4)

The history of the freight lines brings us to the origins of Garland's name. There are several stories about this. One of them says the town was named for Ed and Charles Garland, who ran freight from the town. Mae Urbank, in her book, *Place Names of Wyoming*, however, claimed it was named for John Garland, a forest ranger. Another story told by Les Lawrence, said that some people thought the name came from the Garland Stove, an old range model used by many people, at the turn of the century.

Garland could have been officially named "The Gate City," if Anselmo B. Smith had had his way. Mr. Smith was an agent for the Lincoln Land Co., and he surveyed the townsite in 1901. Although "The Gate City" was not chosen as the official name, the title stuck, and Garland became known as "Garland, Wyoming, The Gate City." It was a fitting title, as Garland is the gateway to the Bighorn Basin.

Although there is no concrete evidence, the strongest theories lean toward the idea that the town was named after the Garland brothers. A newspaper article found in Irma Yont's collection states that, "Garland began in the late 1800s as a watering hole for the horses pulling overland freight wagons. A freighter, Charlie Garland, broadened further this wide spot in the road by laying out a town." (NA2) No one is sure if the credit for doing so should go to Charles Garland or to Anselmo Smith, but Ed and Charles were probably the first to erect a building there. They built a warehouse, using, interestingly enough, square nails called "cut nails." Its purpose was to store freight until it could be hauled to the railheads or picked up by Bighorn Basin residents who had ordered it. The freighters moved

A freight team hauling goods from Worland, Wyoming to Garland, Wyoming. Photo courtesy of Fred Lang.

items from the railheads to Garland's warehouse, where they were stored until they were picked up. (I16) When the railroad came, the tracks were only about 50 feet from the Garland Brothers' warehouse. To keep it in service, the siblings built a ramp to the railroad which made it easy to unload freight from the train into the building. The building's location made it desirable for wool growers. After the Garland Brothers moved out, new tenants converted the building into a wool shed where wool was stored until it could be shipped out on the railroad. In the early 1950s, the first building was torn down. (I6) The Garland brothers, who apparently had greater ambitions, did not stay in the community they had put on the map. They relocated to Burlington before 1905 where they ran a freight, coach, and livery business. (I16)

Garland was a watering hole for freighters, ranchers, and other travelers passing through the area. About a quarter mile from where the Bitter Creek runs through the town, the creek splits and forms a small island. A corral was built on the island for people traveling with horses through Garland. They could keep their horses in the corral while they fed and watered them. (I21) Sometimes, even shepherds drove their sheep through Garland on their way to the mountains in the summer and back through on their way to their winter range. (I19)

Although the water drew people to the area, in the beginning the water supply was not dependable, and its quality was poor. At times, the water level in Bitter Creek was 17 to 18 feet deep, but there were other times, during the late summer, when there was barely a trickle. This didn't change until the Powell Flat was irrigated and the waste water was dumped into Bitter Creek. (I16) To help maintain a steady, dependable supply of water, the people of Garland decided to put a well right in the middle of the main intersection. At first, they dug 90 feet deep, but they found no water. Still believing they were in the right place, they drilled an additional 60 feet and were finally successful. The water was pumped out by a windmill and used for freight teams and stock belonging to the local residents, but it was not fit for human consumption. It had too many minerals and a strong, unpleasant flavor. (B9)

The windmill that pumped water out of the well for freight teams and stock. Photo courtesy of the Park County Historical Archives.

For their personal use, the townspeople were forced to depend upon the water hauled by the railroad, which also required a good source of non-alkaline water for its trains, depot agents, and section crews. (NA8) To solve all these problems, the railroad hauled water from Scribner, a flagstop with a section house and water tank near Warren. (B11) It was put into the railroad cistern at Garland, where the residents could purchase it for a small fee. (I16)

Of interest is a related article from *The Garland Guard,* July 21, 1905:

Pay Your Water Rent

At the special water meeting held last Saturday, the following arrangements and readjustment of water rent rates were agreed upon:

D.A. McCulloch was appointed treasurer, and those using water from the cistern are requested to make the payment of the amount set opposite their respective names to Dave McCulloch, no later than the 15th of each month, and the treasurer is to turn the amount over to Agent Norton on the 16th of every month, together with the names of any who failed to pay, against whom the cisterns will be locked until payment by said delinquents is made.

Note – It is not required that a house to house collection shall be made by the treasurer, but each and every water user must make payment to the treasurer in person.

Following is the list of those who are using water and the amount set opposite the respective names:

Gate City Hotel	$3.00
Garland Hotel	$3.00
Kelly's Restaurant	$2.00
Garland Merc. Co.	$1.50
Garland Lumber Co.	$1.50
Thomas Long, Res	$1.00
C.B. King, Res	$1.00
C.A. Sarver, Res	$1.00
D.A. McCulloch, Res	$1.00
E.C. Spencer, Res	$1.00
Chas. E. Birks, Res	$1.00
Ora Allen, Res	$1.00
Art Crandall, Res	$1.00
Emil Vaterlaus, Res	$1.00
J.F. Lampman, Res	$1.00
J.H. Nevill, Res	$1.00
"Dad" Frasure, Res	$1.00
S.C. Ferdig, Res	$1.00
Total	$25.00 (NP1)

The water rent schedule ran several times in *The Garland Guard.* Burchel Hopkin believes his grandmother, who ran the Garland Hotel, regularly sent his dad, or one of the other boys, to the cistern with a wooden barrel, placed on a sled and pulled behind a team of horses. He thought they had done this every few days as they ran out of water. (I16) Earl Jones reports that the water at their place was no good. He could remember going down to get ten gallons of water "darn near every day from that cistern." (I17) The residents of Garland must have approved of the system, as there were no complaints found in the newspaper. They were, however, glad to see the windmill go.

On November 11, 1905, *The Garland Guard* reported that "the Burlington Railroad Company intends to put in a gasoline engine, at this point, at the site of the present town pump windmill system, which has been an eyesore to the public and a nuisance, too, if ever there was one. The company can't push the work any too fast to suit the public." (NP1)

On December 9, 1905, another article ran in *The Garland Guard.*

New Power for Town Pump

F.T. Bitzner, representing the International Harvester Co. of America, was in town this week and while here, superintended the installation of one of the celebrated International Harvester Company's gasoline engines to supplant the old windmill power plant. The new power source is already installed and is in successful operation, much to the satisfaction of the long-suffering public.

The company is prepared to put in engines and centrifugal pumps for irrigation purposes. The gasoline engines seem to be the coming power. They are used for many different purposes. Up to date, this company has sold but few engines, for the reason that no make of gasoline engines has, as yet, proved anywhere near perfection, but now they have attained that degree of perfection that they are a success wherever installed." (NP1)

In 1916, Dave Wasden and his dad, J.B. Wasden, filled in the old well. (I16)

Besides the availability of water, land was another resource that drew people to Garland. The early settlers were individuals who were convinced that Garland was going to be the town to cater to the influx of people coming to develop the land. They didn't even seem to be concerned when they learned that the railroad was branching off to serve other parts of the Basin. Their optimism was present in every edition of *The Garland Guard.*

June 16, 1905 – Garland can boast of more old bachelors than any other town in the United States, in proportion to population, and all on the mash, too. It also has its troublesome spinsters, and these are also on the mash.

June 23, 1905 – Houses are springing up as if by magic all over the beautiful Garland flat, and what it is now doing is but a forerunner of that which is to be later. When these lands are again open to entry, Garland has a magnificent future before her.

September 8, 1905 – Everything now points to an immediate era of activity and prosperity in this vicinity. From NOW on, watch us grow.

October 14, 1905 – As an immediate result of the early commencement of all kinds of work, business in Garland is looking up, at present, and indications are that it will continue.

December 9, 1905 **Garland Busy Town Now**
Some of our neighboring settlements thought they were justified in giving Garland the boss laugh when it became known that the Burlington had decided to branch off at Frannie instead of Garland. Many made slurring and insinuating remarks concerning our town, claiming that the move on the part of the B&M would kill Garland deader than a door nail.

Not only has this prediction proven false, but the exact opposite is the fact. Whole trainloads of men are being shipped in from various parts of the Union, who are put to work as fast as contractors can put them on. It's outside money that keeps up the town. The company has established a huge commissary here, and the contractors all along the line will receive their supplies from this point. All these many hundreds of men disembark here and remain for several days before going out on the grade.

The hotels of Garland, three in number, are crowded to their utmost capacity. The Garland Mercantile Company and the Garland Lumber and Hardware Company have been compelled to increase their work force; the Garland Meat Market is the busiest place in town, and the Garland State Bank has the money on deposit which will pay off the large force monthly. Garland citizens are extremely happy, while our neighbors, who were praising the powers that be for the railroad giving us the marble heart, as they thought, are in a jealous rage and green with envy because of our good fortune. And the fact of the matter is that Garland is an exceedingly busy town.

December 16, 1905 **Boost for Garland**
Don't knock. Now, then. A long pull,strong pull and a pull altogether for the advancement of our booming new town. Well, what about a dollar dinner? Get busy, citizens of Garland, if you want to make of this town what it is destined to be. Other towns are pulling for their own, and we have got to do the same for Garland if we want to keep up with the procession.

January 21, 1906 **Boost for Garland**
A great many opportunities present themselves for Garland businessmen to 'boost' for the town. It is up to them to say whether or not Garland shall become a good town.

Now is the time to get together and plan for the future. We are reliably informed that the land on the Garland Flat is soon to be open for entry again, when the rush of home-seekers will begin in earnest, and this, together with the fact that the Government project near Corbett is already well underway, which will furnish water for irrigation and domestic purposes, ought to be sufficient incentive for our businessmen to arrange to capture the increased trade, which is bound to follow.

The Guard has long been trying to work up a sentiment in favor of a "Dollar Dinner" where these questions could be discussed and plans laid in advance of the certain influx of newcomers.

It is easy to see that a town could spring up "in a night," as it were, at Ralston, which with wide-awake, progressive businessmen, might do Garland all kinds of mischief. Let's get up and become busy. (NP1)

Even though the citizenry may have been afraid that another town could be built and could take away their plans, it was probably only a matter of fleeting concern. It is strange that by 1905, the town of Garland, having approximately 300 people living there, seemed to be waiting and preparing for the people they knew the opening of the Garland Flat would bring. Construction on the Garland Canal wasn't scheduled to begin until the next year. What were they all doing? Were they all so certain the canal system would be completed, that it would be a success, and that it would be all that was necessary to encourage people to come to this dry part of the country? Does the same level of optimism exist in today's society? Garland's pioneers had the faith that soon people would come. Their certainty is illustrated in this article found in *The Garland Guard* from June 2, 1906, which promoted their town and the Big Horn Basin.

The Gate City

Garland is situated on the branch of the Burlington Railway which taps the Big Horn Basin. It lies in the heart of the Shoshone Project of the Reclamation Service, U.S.G.S. Surrounding it are 100,000 acres of the best land that lies outdoors. This will be irrigated next season by one of the best ditches ever built. Crops that never fail in a climate that is unsurpassed are two conditions hard to beat. We have them. They will make a city and community where all will be prosperous and happy. There are plenty of chances here for the poor man and the investor "to get in on the ground floor." You had better grasp the opportunity. The Big Horn Basin is the coming section of the West. Here lies an undeveloped empire, full of natural resources. The National Government, as well as numerous wealthy individuals and corporations, are furnishing the money to develop it rapidly. These projects are going to put land within the reach of home builders. If you want to invest your money where it is well secured and sure to double in a short time, if you want to find a country where you can earn a home that will support you in affluence, if you want to live in the finest climate under the sun while doing it, come to the Big Horn Basin. (NP1)

Even though the Garland Canal was not completed until 1909, the Garland Division was open for homesteading November 25, 1907. (MS,EX 18) The people who lived in Garland still had faith that the water situation would be rectified and that the Garland Flat would prosper.

Coming to the Garland area to claim land was not easy. The terrain was much different than that to which the new homesteaders were accustomed. It took some getting used to.

Wanda Hart tells the story of her mom's arrival on the train in 1907. Her mother was from North Dakota and was heartbroken when she observed what was in front of her. She had come from a pretty valley, with trees and a river, to a place offering nothing but alkali. Wanda's mother met her father shortly thereafter, which, thankfully, improved the situation. They were married in December of 1908. (I12) Herb Jones's grandmother also arrived on the train. She moved here to live with her husband and had similar feelings about the Garland Flats. Their home was a framed "shack," as Herb puts it. "Grandma came out here, and shortly after that, Grandpa went hunting. The snow blew inside, and she was ready to go back to Illinois unless he built her a house." (I18) Wanda was glad to report that despite her initial reaction, her mother and Herb's grandmother got used to the area and eventually called it home.

Dave Wasden had a much different experience. After traveling a roundabout way from central Utah, he knew, from the beginning, that Garland was "home."

"The route took us first to Denver, then Alliance Nebraska, Newcastle Wyoming, past the coke ovens at Cambria, and on to Toluca, where we boarded the train for Cody."

He arrived in Garland December 6, 1904, the night of his sixth birthday. He saw it as sort of a promised land and always felt it was something special. (M,A,&P 9)

Some people considered Garland to be their home, while others used it as a jumping off point into the Bighorn Basin. There were several ways for them to get to Garland, some easier than others. David Edwin Basset and his family joined a caravan and came into the Bighorn Basin in 1900. They brought all of their possessions in covered wagons, trailing the horses and cattle behind. Arriving at the Shoshone River, near present-day Penrose, just south of the town of Garland, they were first introduced to salt sage, in lieu of grasses. When Eliza climbed out of the wagon and could see no grass for the cows, she said, "Ed, you surely aren't going to camp here. There is no feed for the cows." Ed replied that the cows could eat the salt sage. (B1)

On March 9, 1905, late in the evening, an immigrant train arrived in Garland from Clarkson, KY. Aboard were 20 people on their way to take up homesteads in Worland. All 20 stayed at the Hopkin Hotel their first two nights. The hotel did not have enough beds and bedding available, so the homesteaders took blankets from their immigrant cars and fashioned beds for the children where ever space was available. The women and children continued to live under these conditions for two weeks while the men explored the area and bought horses and wagons to take the party to Worland. Once underway, it took three days to get there. Some traveled by wagon and some traveled by stage.

An early Garland home. Photo courtesy The Powell Tribune. *June 14, 1959.*

Mrs. Clara (S.A. Wortham) Green remembers of that adventure that the Hopkin Hotel was across the tracks from the Garland Depot. She also recalls that, at that time, Garland had, besides the depot, a post office, hotels, a church, a lumberyard, a grocery store, several taverns, and many residents living there. (MA&P 3)

Katie Brown reminisces about her parents and of the way they got to Garland. It is a story she doesn't often tell.

"My mother's parents felt that Henry (my dad) wasn't good enough for their daughter, but my parents continued to see each other anyway. They corresponded for three years (and) then decided to get married. Henry came to Chicago. (He was a Catholic, and she was a Methodist, so we are all little "bastards" because they had to be married by a justice of the peace. I'm just saying it like they told us. They came out here. People were coming out here to homestead, and they had half a train car full of their things. Mom came on the train because she could get a pass. Dad came with their belongings. He had a cow, a dozen chickens, a dog, and their belongings. When he got to Omaha, he had had enough of that, so he kicked the dog out, let the chickens go, sold the cow, and jumped on the freight train, a good old freight train to get here."

A lot of people arrived in Garland with only the knowledge they had gleaned from advertisements put out by the Burlington Railroad. Some came to Garland in immigrant cars. John Hendricks came aboard an immigrant car from Mt. Vernon, Indiana. The car was loaded with 108 colonies of bees ($4/colony), bee equipment, a tent, a bed and bedding, a table and chairs, a stove, cooking utensils, and dishes. (B4) Earl Jones' granddad also rented an immigrant car. He brought his horses, and their feed, seed, and household goods. (I17) The train stopped in Garland. When the immigrants arrived with all of their worldly possessions, Tom Johnson met them at the train. He ran what locals called "sucker wagons." They called the immigrants from the East "suckers" because they bought land without knowing what they were getting. Mr. Johnson took them out to show them plots of land and farms, after which Earl reports they went to Powell to the spot where Nelson Insurance is now located. There used to be a government house there, and the way Earl understood it, agents held drawings. Hoping to get the land they had chosen, the easterners gathered around the porch. (I17)

Home seekers on the Burlington Railroad at Frannie, Wyoming. Shoshone Irrigation District photo archives.

As soon as people found what they were looking for, they began developing the area. There were many firsts to follow. Earl Jones relates that he was born in the first house built on the flat. It was constructed by Dr. Robinson, a physician for the railroad. (I17) O.G. Norton, an early railroad agent, was the first to file for homestead rights on the Powell project; he moved to Garland in 1903. (NA7) Two more of the first townsmen to arrive in Garland were James W. Beatly and Thomas Long of Newcastle, Wyoming. They had business connections with L.A. Gantz, a sheepman of Casper, Wyoming and A.L. Putman. Together they started the Garland Mercantile Co. Thomas Long served as a notary public as well as performed store duties. He also dabbled in real estate, offering Garland town lots for sale. The first land broken by plow on the Garland Flat belonged to Thomas Long, who had filed on a homestead south of Garland. The work was done by Charlie Miller of Byron in 1908. Mr. Long also built a seven-room log house during that time. (I28)

For many of the homesteaders, the Flats provided their first experience with irrigation. Before they set out for Wyoming, they had been advised to bring enough capital and supplies to sustain themselves for one year, until their land was productive. (B9) They expected to pay only nominal costs. In 1908, land was going for just $45 per acre, with operation and maintenance fees of an additional $1. The farmers who were working the land soon felt, however, that they had been misinformed. They argued that they had been led to believe that their farms would prosper as soon as water came, though the promoters probably had not intentionally led them astray.

When newcomers arrived, they also found that they would have to build up the soil. In order to do this, they began to grow alfalfa and sweet clover and add organic fertilizers. At the time they were

Home seekers riding in "sucker wagons." Photo courtesy of Fred Lang.

doing this, they were also supposed to be paying Reclamation Fees, but it was hard to come up with money when they didn't have crops to sell. (B2)

In 1910, more bad news was added to the mix. Of the 15,000 acres irrigated in the Powell and Garland area, 10,000 acres were damaged by flooding. The land was severely over-watered, and the water table had crept into the root zone of the crops. Alkali began to form, cellars were flooded, fields were just too wet, and they began to bog. A team of agricultural engineers came to analyze the situation. They decided that the farmers were to blame because they were "using too much water" on the fields. The engineers recommended that drains be installed to lower water levels and keep them down. This was an expense the Reclamation Service had not planned on, so the cost was passed on to the farmers. In the fall of 1911, work on the open and tile drains began, and, for the next several years, the farmers and the Reclamation Service went round and round. The federal agency wanted to be paid, but the farmers didn't know how to pay them, since they didn't have any crops to sell. (B2) Many farmers were forced out, but some managed to make it work.

Katie Brown tells the story of the way her dad managed when money was tight.

"We only had a 40-acre farm, so my dad always worked extra. He worked at the alfalfa mill and drove the school wagon. He always did extra things. One thing he did; he was a good poker player. He would do the chores, so he could leave on Friday morning, play poker till Sunday morning, and be back before church; he never slept or drank. He wore bib overalls with a pocket on top for his poker money. And when Momma needed money for the groceries, or the baby needed diapers, she would get [his poker winnings] from there. It was like a business for him, a way to get extra money to feed his family. I can remember him walking to town, after my aunt had sent him a policeman's fur coat, and he went to play poker. We could hardly wait for him to get back because, he would have boxes; it seems to me, the boxes were big, great big boxes of chocolates with beautiful ladies' pictures on them. Maybe sometimes he didn't win anything or didn't have enough money to buy any candy, but when he did, we were in hog heaven. He played poker, so we weren't hungry, and I never thought it was bad." (I2)

Gambling apparently was a popular pastime and a way for people to increase their income. Even though Katie didn't think it was bad, some of the community members did, as can be seen in the following articles from *The Garland Guard*.

March 17, 1906 – Dave McCulloch, this week posted a notice that henceforth no more gambling for money would be tolerated at the Gate City Saloon, and he wishes it understood that the lid is down tight and on to stay. Dave is to be commended upon his decision in voluntarily stomping on evil that, at best, is a pernicious habit. He has always been on the side of law and order, and the people respect him for it.

March 31, 1906 – His Honor, Judge Parmalee will be kept exceedingly busy with the horde of gamblers that have been run in during the past two weeks.

April 7, 1906 – Sheriff Fenton has issued rigid orders closing all the gambling joints in the Basin. Drunks galore these days and fights by the score. Some of our wet goods merchants have evidently a peculiar brand of fighting booze. We would like to know just who sells it – it would be the boss stuff to give to delinquent subscribers. And now the lid is down tight once more, throughout the Basin. It is said that 150 gamblers have been arrested and that all these will be hauled up before his Honor, Judge Parmalee, at the coming April term of court. Screw the lid down tight, so she'll stay. (NP1)

Gambling was not the only socially unacceptable activity going on in Garland in the early years. According to Ted Lord, Garland was pretty rough. Men were shot, there was a "happy" house, and at least three saloons (or as many as seven), and drunkenness was a concern of the Garland residents. There are many stories about Garland that never were recorded, but enough trouble was brewing that a justice of the peace was installed to try to keep some kind of order in the rough, little town.

December 2, 1905

It is Now Judge Miller

Some time ago, Judge James F. Lampman resigned his office as Justice of The Peace for Garland precinct, on account of his removal to Cody.

At the last sitting of the Board of County "Daddies," Mr. Chas. F. Miller, the popular barkeeper at the Gate City Saloon, was appointed to serve out the unexpired term, and if he qualifies for the position, Garland will again have a splendid peace officer. The appointment of Mr. Miller is a happy one, as he is especially well qualified for the office. We believe he will uphold the dignity of the law, in all respects, and as to his judgment upon legal points, that is altogether on the side of the right. We believe that time will prove the wisdom of the board's action in making this excellent appointment.

Mr. Miller has established himself in Garland, being one of the first to comply with the provisions of The Homestead Law. He is now living out on his homestead. (NP1)

Many believe that the reason Garland died, and that Powell came to life was because of the saloons and the wildness of the smaller town. Some say that when the Reclamation Project came to the area, its office couldn't be built within five miles of a saloon. Garland wouldn't give up its saloons, so the Reclamation office moved to Powell. After that, the story goes that the people started to migrate toward Powell, and Garland began to fade.

There is some evidence that backs up this story. Robert Bonner, in his book, *Farm Town, Stories of the Early History of Powell*, addresses this issue. He points out the 1893 Wyoming statute prohibiting the sale of liquor within five miles of a site where 25 or more men were employed in a labor of public construction. The thinking behind that was that it would make for more productive workers if those workers were not affected by over-exposure to alcohol. Bonner goes on to point out that Shoshone Project contractors had stipulated that the Reclamation Service would provide an environment in which intoxicants could not be purchased. Determined entrepreneurs tried to set up saloons for hard-working, thirsty workers anyway, but their licenses were usually revoked. The entrepreneurs, who knew their way around the system, were bought out by the Reclamation Service to satisfy the demands of the contractors. (B2)

Aside from the issue of the saloons, the center of the project was declared to be a more equitable location. (B9) So, Camp Coulter was established along the railroad, in the middle of the flat, in the summer of 1907. Its name was changed to Powell in 1908 and it continued to be a family-oriented place with temperance ordinances firmly in place. Powell continued to be a dry community until 1934. (B2)

It would not be accurate to say that Garland's decline was entirely due to actions of the government. Local businessmen and residents had their part in it too. Burchell Hopkin says that some of the merchants thought they had a corner on the market and expected to profit from all the development that they thought would take place, so they inflated their land prices. Hopkin reiterates: "They were trying to speculate a little too heavily and speculated themselves right out of existence."

The townspeople of Garland did not take this lying down. They didn't want Powell to grow at their expense, and neither did William F. Cody (though Cody's interest was primarily in Ralston). Congressman Frank Mondell received letters from Cody and petitions from Garland residents against the incorporation of Powell as a town site. (B2) The letter-writing and petitions didn't work, however, and the city of Powell was established. Garland bravely continued to strive toward the future.

Over the years, the town experienced boom and bust until eventually, it became what you see today. The residents of Garland, though much reduced in number, are still an optimistic sort, telling and retelling the stories that formed its colorful history.

Chapter 2 - The Train: Bringing Life to Garland

The railroad not only brought water and people to Garland; it also brought life. Some might say the railroad is what made Garland; others don't agree. However, the railroad did help Garland to boom. In the beginning, it brought the people; it brought the mail, and it brought all the supplies that people needed in order to live. It was an important part of community life and always a fascination to the children.

The Big Horn Southern Railroad Company, which would eventually run the branch line from Toluca to Cody, was incorporated under the laws of the Montana Territory, December 20, 1888. (B9) On November 22, 1892, the first train arrived in Sheridan, Wyoming, on the tracks built by the Burlington Railroad. By October 3, 1894, the tracks had extended to Huntley, Montana, where the Burlington Railroad met with the Northern Pacific Line. (B11) By 1899, Buffalo Bill Cody was able to interest the Burlington Railroad in constructing a line from Toluca, Montana, to Cody, Wyoming. (B12) Edward Gillette was sent out to survey the route, which would run south from Toluca toward Pryor, through the Gap, down Sage Creek, and then turn southwest, toward Cody, at Frannie. (B11) 131 miles of railroad line from Toluca to Cody was located. (B9)

According to Paul Weaver, in his *A History of Frannie*, the name Toluca was attributed to a wandering Swede who, upon arriving at the end of the line, got off the train and ambled about wide-eyed until he was asked if he was looking for someone. He replied, "Oh no! I yust come to looka." And so the name of the Toluca line has stuck for all time. (MS10)

To cross the Crow Reservation, the railroad had to receive special permission from the Crow Nation. (B9) Each of the Indian allottees, whose land was to be crossed, was given a map to show

The Toluca Depot along "The Squaw Line." Photo courtesy of Fred Lang.

where the railroad would come through. General Charles F. Manderson, the line's general counsel, felt that this was a waste of time, but seeing no way around it, had an interpreter accompany their employee responsible for distributing the maps, to explain what was going on. (B12) The section of line from Toluca to Cody was called the "Squaw Line," as over half of it went through the reservation. (B9)

Construction of the Toluca to Cody line started in the spring of 1900. (B11) It is a little known fact, except to students of Bighorn Basin history, that the Mormon colonists had a huge impact on the construction of the Toluca to Cody rail line. The colonists were in the area working on the Sidon Canal when they were contracted to build 23 miles of railroad line from the Pryor Gap Tunnel to Scribner (near Warren). The Mormon leaders split the colonists into three groups. One group built houses; one worked on the canal, and the third worked on the railroad. (B9) By October of 1900, 90 percent of the men in the Cowley colony had been subcontracted to construct the railroad. They took their families and lived in camps along the railroad right of way. There was a Tie Camp at the top of the Pryor Mountains, on the west end, where workers hand-hewed ties for the railroad. The largest camp was on Sage Creek, at the head of Pryor Gap. During the winter of 1900, typhoid fever hit the camp, and many people were confined to bed; many others attended the sick, and construction on the railroad slowed. Most people recovered, but there were possibly two or three deaths. After the work was completed at Pryor Gap, the camp moved to Coyote Creek, and, by late spring, to the Jack Morris Ranch near Frannie. The colonists received $90,000 for their labor. (B7)

William F. Cody was instrumental in the completion of the railroad. He offered the railroad right of way across the Shoshone Irrigation Company. He also donated additional lands in Cody because the railroad would provide the most efficient means of hauling necessary materials for construction of the Buffalo Bill Dam. He had his eye on tourism as well. (I13) The Lincoln Land Company (incorporated in 1880) was not part of the railroad but worked closely with the Burlington line. Its main purpose was to develop communities at fairly regular intervals along the railroad. The Lincoln Land Company demanded one half the townsite as its price and paid the Shoshone Land Company just $10 per acre for the property. The following is a list of the Lincoln Land Company townsites along the Squaw Line and other spurs that were built later: Cody, Corbett, Cowley, Durkee, Garland, Greybull, Kane, Lovell, Lucerne, Manderson, Neiber, Otto, Rairden, and Ralston. (B12) The first train to Cody came through November 11, 1901. Colonel Cody was on it. It was followed by a Billings Special with Senator Clarence Don Clark aboard. (B12)

In the five years after the train arrived, Garland was booming. It was a railhead, but in 1905, there was some concern that this could change. Rumor had it that a new line was to be built. Some thought that it might branch at Garland, while others felt this would happen in Frannie. If it branched in Garland, the community would continue to grow. Travelers would require housing and eating establishments, and residents would need places to purchase supplies. If the railroad branched elsewhere, it would take business away from Garland. The following is an article, relative to this dilemma, found in *The Garland Guard* in 1905:

Railroad Men Have Complete Tour of Inspection – General Manager Holdrege Interviewed by
Representative of *The Guard*. But is Noncommittal –
Well pleased with the Big Horn County and its Resources General Manager Holdrege and a party

of Burlington officials left for the East, on their Special, on Wednesday at 1:30 p.m. Just before pulling out, *The Guard* man managed to have a brief interview with Mr. Holdrege, but, as usual, he was noncommittal with regard to the proposed extension of the Burlington. On other matters, he talked quite freely. When asked if he had anything to say for publication, he said: "You may say that we are much pleased with our trip, with what we have seen and with the treatment accorded us by the people of the Basin. With regard to the extension of our line, I am not prepared to say what will be done; that depends entirely upon the action of the Board of Directors after our report shall have been submitted. We are going east now for that purpose. I cannot say at what point the road will branch off; that will be determined when it is decided whether to make the extension or not." (NP1)

Construction of the line from Frannie to Thermopolis began October 3, 1905, dooming the Cody line to become only a branch. The extended line was welcomed by inhabitants of the Bighorn Basin. To them, it meant that the time it took to receive freight would be shortened considerably, so the line couldn't be built fast enough to suit them. It reached Worland on July 10, 1906. (B9) By 1907, it connected to Kirby. At this point, spurs were built to serve the coal mine at Gebo. (B12) Heading south through the Wind River Canyon, to the Burlington track, it finally arrived in Thermopolis May 13, 1910. In 1914, the tracks continued to Orin Junction and tied into the line that went on to Denver. (B11) Residents of the Basin now had a more efficient way of obtaining their goods. No longer did they have to spend days freighting to and from Garland.

In the meantime, railroad engineers decided they needed an easier route to Warren from Billings, so, in 1909, they began to build a track from Fromberg, Montana, which was the end of the Northern Pacific spur. The new line passed through Bridger and the Jack Creek Valley, over the Divide, and into Frannie. It was a more direct route for passengers and freight. (B11) It shortened the line and eliminated the heavy grade through Pryor Gap. (B9) The water tank and section house at Scribner's was moved one mile south to Warren, the new flagstop. The first train to travel on the new route came through April 24, 1911. The Toluca line was then abandoned and the tracks torn up, almost overnight, in May of that same year. (B11)

The train that came through Garland in those early years was powered by a steam locomotive. The speed limit was 30 m.p.h. for a mixed train, with both freight and passenger cars, and 25 m.p.h. for one carrying just freight. (B9) Later, speeds would change as loads diversified and became heavier.

At first, the train arrived three times a week from Toluca. Mrs. Stout remembered seeing bags tagged for Basin, Greybull, Manderson, Hyattville, Shell, and Germania. The mail was loaded on a cart at the depot and housed at the post office until the next day. Then it was loaded on the stagecoach for delivery to the Bighorn Basin towns. Mrs. Stout's father, O.G. Norton, was the first station agent at the Garland Depot and the first to file on a homestead. (NA 1)

In the beginning, the Toluca to Cody train was slow, as the tracks were built quickly and were rough. The train still made it much easier for Garland residents to get around though, to receive goods, and to send out freight. However, the schedule was not very dependable. This shortcoming was mentioned several times in *The Garland Guard*. The newspaper either criticized or praised the trains, depending on their ability to keep up the schedule. The following are among the comments made about the train's punctuality - or lack of it:

August 11, 1905 – Trains are again running most wretchedly irregular these days, owing no doubt to the operators' strike on the Northern Pacific.

October 7, 1905 – Trains are coming in any old time of late.
November 18, 1905 – Trains are running frightfully irregular of late, much to the disgust of the traveling public.

February 24, 1906 – Trains on the Cody branch have been running more nearly on time this week. A great improvement is noticeable.

May 12, 1906 – Trains on the Cody branch have been running on excellent time during the past two weeks. (NP1)

The railroad continued to try to keep to its schedule. The management made changes, as the demand required it.

December 2, 1905 – Trains on the Cody branch are now making about two trips a week. No mail from Cody Wednesday and none from the East on Tuesday. One of the engines is in cold storage in the yards here, immovable as the Rock of Gibraltar. How long must we put up with such a state of affairs?

February 3, 1906 – On the 11th, a new timeline will go into effect on the Toluca – Cody Branch. Instead of the train leaving Cody at 11:20 p.m. as it now does, it will depart from there about 9:30 p.m., arriving at Garland about 10:30 p.m. West bound, instead of arriving here at 4:40 p.m., it will arrive at this point about 1:30 p.m. This will be a great improvement over the present schedule. A person having business in Cody can leave early in the afternoon, having several hours in Cody, and return home in the early evening.

February 17, 1906 – The new train schedule now in force seems to be working both ways. Part of the time, they are running on the old schedule, and part of the time, they are trying to come up to the new one. As to the latter, they have signally failed so far, and part of the time, they even shame the old schedule. What's the matter, anyhow?

June 30, 1906 – *The Guard* is informed, from a reliable source that train service between Toluca and Worland will consist of four passenger trains per day. The train service will doubtless not be changed, between Frannie and Cody, from the present schedules. (NP1)

There were some problems over which the railroad simply had no control. Accidents and weather kept the train from coming in on schedule from time to time. Human error was also the cause on some occasions.
March 24, 1906 – Trains have become demoralized due to recent storms and cold weather and are again running on any kind of schedule.

December 2, 1905 – "Freight Wreck East of Garland" A small freight wreck occurred yesterday morning near Mantua. Particulars were about as follows: A freight train, eastbound, pulled out of Garland about 7 a.m., and when near Mantua the engine ran out of water. The engine was run to Crockett and filled. It was running back onto the train on a steep grade, when within a few hundred yards of the cars, the engineer applied the brake so as to get down onto the train easy. He discovered that instead of slowing up, owing to the frozen rails, the engine was gaining speed very fast. He at once reversed the engine, but all to no purpose. She still went on, faster and faster, until, all at once, [they were] sideways across the track. No one was hurt, a most remarkable thing, all things considered. The engineer and fireman had placed themselves in such a position that they were able to escape when the crash came. (NP1)

December 30, 1905 – An extra on the Cody branch was wrecked Wednesday morning, going down Pryor hill. The engine, which, with two freight cars, left the track, was demolished, and the fireman was badly scalded about the face and neck, besides being more or less seriously crushed. He was sent to the hospital in Sheridan on No. 42. The engineer escaped uninjured.

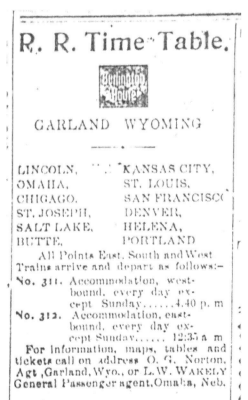

A railroad time table from The Garland Guard, January 6, 1906

December 30, 1905 – The day coach of the train on the Cody Branch was the scene of a disgraceful, drunken brawl on the part of a lot of hoboes. Conductor Merritt soon displayed the stuff that he is made of and in a jiffy, the drunken belligerents were expelled from the car, much to the relief and satisfaction of the other passengers. Conductor Merritt deserves much praise for the prompt manner in which he quelled the disturbance. He is a gentleman of the highest honor, and to know him is to respect him. (NP1)

December 14, 1917 – Mr. Garver, foreman of the Illinois Pipe Line Crew which is unloading pipe here and at Mantua, passed through a painful accident Monday, when he fell from a car loaded with twenty-four pipes. He was brought back here on the noon train and upon examination, the doctor found no broken bones. He was placed under the care of J.M. Cross, who has had several years experience as a nurse, and is doing nicely. (NP2)

People coming to Garland were unaware of the scheduling difficulties and probably were not concerned about it. They were drawn to the area by advertisements similar to the ones found in *The Garland Guard*.

October 7, 1905 – "Burlington Bulletin of Round

Trip Rates"
- Chicago and return, on sale daily - $57.40
- Portland, Tacoma, and Seattle and return - $40.00
- Cheap Home Seekers' rates in many directions - first and third Tuesdays of each month.
- If you will call or write, it will be a pleasure to advise you about rates and train service, to reserve you a berth, and to try to make your trip a comfortable one.
- For further particulars write to or call on O.G. Norton, at Garland, Wy; or L.W. Wake, Ley, G.P. & T.A., Omaha, Neb.

March 17, 1906 – "RR Timetable – Burlington Route – Garland Wyo."

Lincoln	Kansas City
Omaha	St. Louis
Chicago	San Francisco
St. Joseph	Denver
Salt Lake	Helena
Butte	Portland

All points east, south and west. Trains arrive and depart as follows:

No. 311. Accommodation, westbound, every day, except Sunday; leaves Toluca - 7:30 a.m., arrives at Frannie - 12:20 p.m., leaves Frannie 12:45 p.m., arrives at Garland - 1:00 p.m., stops for dinner and leaves at 1:56 p.m., arrives Cody - 3:10 p.m.

No. 312. Accommodation, eastbound, every day, except Sunday; leaves Cody - 9:00 p.m., arrives Garland - 10:15 p.m., leaves Garland - 10:45 p.m., arrives Frannie - 11:30 p.m., arrives Toluca - 5:00 a.m., making connections at Toluca with No's 41 and 44 eastbound, mainline train.

For information, maps, tables, and tickets, call or address O.G. Norton, Agt, Garland Wyo., or L.W. Wakely, General Passenger agent, Omaha, Neb. (NP1)

The people of Garland welcomed the newcomers.

May 12, 1906 – The Burlington has announced that it will continue its cheap home seekers' excursions during the year. This will undoubtedly be the means of bringing many more people into the Basin before the close of the year. Let 'em come; there is plenty of room. (NP1)

The depot was just as important as the trains themselves and oftentimes was the first thing to make an impression on the travelers. Earl Jones relates that depots all looked alike. They were red, with big storerooms and green roofs. There was a platform outside made of brick laid on edge, so employees could easily push steel wagons filled with freight and travelers' personal belongings. The Garland Depot wasn't any different. It was a two story building. Inside, on the lower floor, was a waiting room with a ticket window. There was also a storeroom that had big doors leading into it. Items unloaded from the train were stored there until someone came to claim them. Bonnie Hiller remembers baggage carts out front being used to move baggage and other items to and from the train. Warren Cubbage said that, in the beginning, the depot agent lived in the upper story.

O.G. Norton was the first depot agent. Win Brown, in later years, also ran the depot. Jack VanLake remembered that Mr. Brown often went upstairs, when he wasn't doing much, and played the xylophone. Jack said he was always playing it. Katie Brown recalls that in about 1931, when she graduated from high school, Mrs. Windfree lived upstairs. Katie's sister, Ethel Heimer, had only been in it once but remembers it was a nice, big building. It had living quarters on the upper level and a big receiving room on the lower one. She remembers Alice Richards living upstairs later on. In 1949 or 1950, Warren's father bought the old depot and moved it to Powell. He made apartments out of it. You can still pass by the depot building today. It is now located north of the old Powell High School and east of the football field, behind the bleachers. (16)

The depot agent and the passenger conductors of the railroad had many jobs. They were in charge of communication, passenger safety, and baggage handlers. They had to be versatile and do a little bit of everything. The passengers depended on them to make their travels safe and enjoyable. Norman "Pete" Woods reported that the telegraph system was down at the depot. "That young guy who ran the telegraph was also the depot agent." Pete said he was an exceptional guy. "He could visit with you, talk on the telephone, and listen to the telegraph message coming over the wire, all at the same time."

This article from *The Garland Guard* further illustrates this point:

March 10, 1906 – Two passenger conductors, now on duty on the Cody branch, Messers. Rhinenuth and Wright, are the most sociable, affable, and accommodating gentlemen ever

The Garland train depot. August 17, 1924. Photo courtesy of Norman "Pete" Woods.

employed on this line. They are pleasant and agreeable young men, have already made a legion of admiring friends, and, without a doubt, are the two handsomest boys on the Burlington system. It is a pleasure to know them, and we hope they will remain on this run always.

The depot agent had several different jobs, but his habits became the fodder for many pranks. Vern Fales remembers one from his childhood.

"The depot master often went out around the depot to take a little afternoon nap. Warren and I sneaked in there after he was asleep and, one day, swiped his pipe. We dumped the ashes out in our hands, filled it about half-full of gunpowder from 22 shells, tamped the tobacco back in, and put it back where we found it. When the depot master lit it, you can imagine what happened! We were long gone, but he knew who did it. For some reason, anything that was done in Garland we were blamed for whether we were responsible or not. But, in all honesty we had done most of it."

Another incident was reported in *The Powell Tribune* on August 10, 1917: Last Thursday morning, while Mr. Norton, our genial depot agent, was in town after the mail, a thief came to the depot and took his bicycle. Mr. Norton missed it as soon as he returned and started a search for it. Upon inquiry, he found a man had just left town on a bicycle. Mr. Jones, Mr. Splawn, and Mr. Norton got in to a car and took after him. When the fellow saw them, he dropped the bicycle and gave them quite a chase before they got him. He was taken to Powell and forced to pay a fine.

There were other railroad facilities, in addition to the depot, that were equally important in shipping freight. Beside the depot sat the most important facility for the train, the water tower. Since the water in Garland was alkaline and hard on the steam engines, the railroad had to haul its own water. The company brought the water to Garland and pumped it into the water tower. The railroad men filled the steam engines with it. This made Garland an important water stop for the steamers. (I6)

There was also a coal tipple used by the railroad. A track was built upon an overhead structure, so the cars could be pulled up there to dump coal into a bin. (I116) Other facilities were also built to help export goods out of the Basin. The warehouse that the Garland Brothers built (the one that was turned into a wool house close to the depot) was one of them. The wool growers stored wool there until they could ship it out. Les Lawrence thought that the wool house was down by the elevator and maybe the water tank for the train too. Pete Wood recalled that it was close to the depot and remembered the wool wagons rolling into town. They were so full of wool that they filled the entire wool house.

There was a stockyard built right along the tracks. In the beginning, before the railroad reached into the southern parts of the Bighorn Basin, ranchers brought sheep and cattle from as far away as Thermopolis and Worland, instead of trailing them all the way to Billings. The stockyards were a convenient place to hold the livestock until the ranchers could load them on the train and ship them out. Pete Wood remembered the yard as being very primitive, but that it was good place to hold the animals until they could be loaded.

The freight trains coming through Garland became a valuable tool for Garland residents to get other items to and from larger markets, even though there were times that the process might have been slow. On April 21, 1906, *The Garland Guard* reported: "It is truly astonishing to see the immense amount of freight that is being shipped here daily for the various Basin points. What will the freighting for the Basin be, once the railroad is completed in Worland?" (NP1)

Sometimes, Garland residents didn't have much luck in the larger markets. When Pete Woods was

Warren Cubbage and Vern Fales playing as if they are fighting. Photo courtesy of Irma Yonts.

five or six years old, in about 1915, his father shipped a carload of potatoes to Omaha, Nebraska, to sell. The market was poor. Pete's father didn't make any money and had to come up with the money for the freight bill for those "darn spuds," despite the situation. The venture was a total loss. (I27)

As late as 1940, Garland residents were still using the train to receive and send items to larger markets. Jack VanLake's parents and Earl Jones's parents used to take cream down to the depot and set it on the platform. The train came, picked it up, and took it to Denver, where it was made into butter. Jack remembered getting *The Denver Post* and reading the funny papers while he was down there on Saturdays.

The alfalfa mill was also a regular stop in Garland. Bonnie Hiller remembers that hay was ground there because, at the time, the big cities used horses for everything and needed the milled hay to feed them. This building later became the potato house, where the train continued to stop in order to ship out potatoes.

The Park Train is remembered fondly by several Garland residents. Originally, when the line from Toluca to Cody was built, people thought it would continue up the Shoshone Canyon to Yellowstone. That didn't happen, but Cody still became a gateway city to Yellowstone National Park. (MS10) A special train called the Park Train ran from Billings to Cody. A small roundhouse in Frannie which looked like a trolley car housed the train crews stationed there for the Park run. Depending on how many people there were, there may have been one or two trains. The passengers rode the train to Cody, where they got off at the big depot on the north side of the river. Some stayed in the big, very nicely furnished hotel until they caught a ride into the park. (I11) From the depot, they took a stage early on, but in later years, there was a yellow bus for them to ride into the park. Lloyd Killiam remembers, "We always went down to the tourist train, to wave at the tourists." Earl Jones also went to watch the Park Train and remembers it coming through from about 8:00 to 10:00 at night, pulling six or seven cars. Ted Lord thought the Park Train came through at 8 p.m., all summer long.

Besides the Park Train, there was the Galloping Goose, a passenger train that was a convenient means of transportation, taking residents back and forth to Powell, Cody, Garland, and Frannie. Upon arrival in Frannie, passengers were able to board a different train that traveled to other destinations, as well. Merl Fales believes it was self-propelled and wishes he knew what happened to it. He also remembers the family dog yelping every time the Galloping Goose came through town and blew the whistle. Several of the Garland residents interviewed either rode it or know of someone who did.

In June of 1916, Pete Wood was down at the depot to give the young boys of Company C a good send off, as they departed to fight for their country in World War I He recalled it this way:

"The train stopped, and they all got on the train. I can remember standing at the platform, watching those kids go off to war. I remember Pete Smith, and Jim Ervin; quite a few of them were neighbors. I can't remember them all, but there was a real little troop of those young kids who boarded that train to go off to war." (I27)

Bonnie Hiller and Pete Woods both used the Galloping Goose to travel to Powell or Cody. Bonnie doesn't remember what it cost to ride, but she does remember that it was during the Depression and that there were gas rations, making it difficult to just get into the car and go. The Galloping Goose ran every day. Ethel Heimer had this to say about the Galloping Goose:

"You always enjoyed seeing, (I think we called it) the 'mud puddle jumper' or the 'Galloping Goose.' And that was always fun for us kids because it was a little more colorful than most of the American trains. I thought it was pretty neat. The railroad had it on the tracks for quite a few years. I don't know what it was that caused them to discontinue it, maybe just the lack of use."

Fay Smith remembers riding on the train to Billings when she got her tonsils out.

"I actually rode from Garland to Billings on the train once. I thought it was nice. I think the seats were red and a plush of some kind. They were soft, and it was a pleasant ride. We went through Warren and Edgar and Silesia and Laurel. I believe the porter, (do you call them that?) - I believe he was black, but maybe not. You know the one who came through and announced the towns as we went through them. Some of them we stopped at. When we got to Billings, I don't remember especially, but I think Dad took us right over to the doctor's and had our tonsils taken out. Then, I don't know how we got to Aunt Maud's. Maybe there was a taxi or something. Because we had sore throats, we went out there. She wanted to feed us. We asked for tomato soup. I think we were only up there a couple days. We couldn't stay up there long. She had a great, big family and not too much to go on. They didn't have any money. I don't remember the ride coming back, but I'm sure that's [the train is] the only way we got home. And someone would have had to meet us at Garland and drive us to Penrose, one of the hired men [probably]; we always had a hired man." (I25)

Earl Jones's father worked at the sugarbeet factory in Billings in about 1923 or 1924. Earl used the train to get to his grandparents' house from there.

"When I was little, my dad worked at the sugarbeet factory and my parents often sent me by train to my grandparents. The cost was only a nickel. Instead of stopping at Garland, the train always dropped me off at the crossing in front of my grandparents' house. (The house on the corner of HWY 14A and Road 5.)" (I17)

The railroad supplied jobs for some of the young Garland citizens. Lloyd Killiam and Jack VanLake both had stories about their experiences working for the railroad. Jack and his friend Gerald were employed by the railroad one winter, for a couple of months, after they graduated from high school.

"The railroad was putting in a little new track up there. They were laying new rails near Dutcher's Springs and on up to Cody. Old Clarky was the section foreman. We rode the sidecar up to Ralston. I remember it was so 'damn cold' riding that thing. We got on the sidecar at Garland. (I was seventeen or eighteen years old.) The section-hand from Cody, we liked a lot better so we tried to get on his crew because Old Clarky was kind of ornery. My buddy always used to get sick-headed, so we quit riding the side car. Gerald had a car, and we said, 'Hell, we'll drive out there,' and Clarky didn't like that. After we had worked there a month or better, Gerald started getting sick. Clarky said, 'You'd just as well go home and take your friend with ya. I said, 'That's all right with me.' So we quit, or he fired us. "(I26)

Lloyd Killiam worked for the railroad for about nine months after WWII in about 1947.

"A job came up at the railroad station, and I got the job as cashier. The conductor was a real character. The day right before he was going to retire, though, he got smashed between two cars over in Frannie." (I19)

Lloyd recalled that they used to pull 150 – 200 oil cars from the refineries in Cody every day with the train. (He wasn't sure if Husky or Texaco was running them at the time.) Because of the heavy loads, the trains had to run pretty fast. They didn't slow down, as they came through the towns because the engineers knew they had to be going about 65 m.p.h. to have enough speed to pull up the Garland Grade. Lloyd remembers a story about the time when the train didn't make the grade.

"The railroad had a lot of guys who went through college and came out with great ideas about efficiency - efficiency experts, they called them. An efficiency expert and the engineer were on the train one day. The expert came into the station. (His name was Itchybottom, or something. We called him 'Itchybritches.' He was a real character.) They started back from Cody with 150 carloads of oil. (That's a lot of weight.) The engineer was just coming through Powell at 65 m.p.h. Everybody knew that the train came through Powell about the same time every day, about 5:00 in the afternoon. They watched for it like a daily attraction. It was going 65 m.p.h, and then the expert says, 'You have to slow down. You can't go through those crossings at 65 m.p.h. You're supposed to go 30 m.p.h.' (He told the engineer to slow her down to 30 mph.)

The engineer hollered, 'Are you out of your head?'

'No, slow her down.'

The engineer slowed it down, and the train got stuck on the hill. The crew was out, I think, nine or ten hours, something like that, but you could not be out of Frannie longer than that, according to union rules. So, they just tied up the train and stayed on the track. The engineer called in (they had a telephone in the caboose) to Frannie to get another engine to help pull them over the Garland Grade. But, when the other train arrived, it had to be rerouted back through Garland, so it could get a run at the hill. It still couldn't be done at first, even with two engines, but the second run did the trick. When the train got into Frannie, there were a lot of calls to the engineer.

He said, 'It's not my fault. Ichybottom told me to slow down the train, so I slowed down the train.'

The engineer told the division superintendent, 'You sent me this efficiency expert, Mr. Itchybritches. He made me slow the train down, going through Powell, to 30 m.p.h.'

The superintendent said, 'You know you can't make the Garland Grade at that speed.'

The engineer replied back, 'Yeah, I know that. I tried to tell him, but he wouldn't listen. So we didn't make the Garland Grade last night, and we tied up the train.'

It cost the railroad thousands of dollars because the oil didn't get to the refinery on time. (I19)

The train was actually very practical. It also held the fascination of the children in Garland. Wanda Hart said that the sound of the train whistle beckoned her to other places, and she knew that when she grew up, she would travel. Pete Woods had fond memories of the train, too. He remembered a boyhood friend who was deaf, but he could "hear" the vibration of the train.

"Honestly, clear over in the hills before you could ever see it, he came yelling, 'WHOO! WHOO!' He could hear that train before I could, and he was deaf. His name was Bobby Dobbs. His dad ran the Garland State Bank at the time."

Pete was also impressed by the athletic ability of the brakey. It was fascinating to him the way the brakey watched the train pull out. He stood there until the last car came along and then grabbed onto the ladder, hung on to it, and swung around to get on the train. Pete figured someone had to be an athlete to do that.

It was important that the railroad employees have a great sense of humor and pride in their work. They must have known and seen the way the children in the towns they went through watched them. Many of the Garland residents told me stories about the railroad employees. Some stories were fond memories; others were suspicious, and still others had an element of danger to them. Pete Wood remembered the day he got to ride with the engineer, as they were switching cars. It was one of his fondest memories. He could still remember "the engineer waving to me to come over and get into the cab of that old freight engine."

Darwin Franklin remembers being surprised by the steam train:

"When we were playing along the track there, the engineers would open up the steam. It seemed to me like they did it on purpose, but I suppose it was just time to blow off a little steam. Didn't matter much. It made me step back. We were standing along the track when the train came along, and the steam came out. We always blamed it on the railroad. We were playing on the pier. I guess that's what you would call it on the outside of the haymill there. Of course, it was closed up, but we liked to play there. That 'darn train' came along, and the hot water was coming out. I think the men did that on purpose."

Pete Wood also remembered sneaking rides on the train.

"We sometimes went around the back side of the train, and hooked rides on the ladders on the end of the freight cars. We rode until the train got pretty good speed and then jumped off. One time, Marian Cross and I rode that ladder. The train crossed the Bitter Creek on the west edge of town, and by the time we were going to bail off, we were over that darn creek. So we rode it until it got over the bridge on the other side. By that time, the train was moving right along. We thought we'd better jump off. Marian didn't get hurt, but even the inside of my ears was skinned. We either had to jump or ride all the way to Powell and walk back, so we decided to jump."

Bonnie Hiller can remember an incident which occurred while she was returning home after club one day.

"My mother was driving the one-horse buggy. We were letting my aunt off in Garland. This horse was a really antsy one. The freight train was going through with a load of sheep that were all 'baaing' and the horse went wild, with the sounds of all those sheep. My mother could hardly hold that horse so that my aunt could get out of the buggy. It's silly little things like that, which you remember from childhood."

The trains coming through Garland are fondly remembered by the residents and made an impact on their lives. For some, they were a means of transportation, while others saw them as a way to let their imaginations run free. Today the train whistle can still be heard as can the cars crashing together near the ASI Bean Mill. The train still comes through twice a day, if demand requires it, passing through Garland in the morning on its way to Cody and back again heading for Frannie in the afternoon. Like that of the trains before it, the schedule remains varied. (Some things never change.) The trains are still unpredictable, and the children are still fascinated by them.

Chapter 3 - Big Business in Garland, Wyoming

Did Ed and Charles Garland have a vision for the town that came to bear their name when they erected the freight warehouse? Who knows? But through the years, there have been a variety of businesses that called Garland home. In the beginning, being at the end of the railroad line, hotels and saloons were booming businesses. There were even rumors of what Ted Lord referred to as a "Happy Hotel" northeast of town. (I22) As the population grew, other services were needed. Businesses such as the Garland Mercantile, Early's Drug Stores, Lampman's Millinery Store, and The Garland Lumber and Hardware Company were built to supply services to the growing population. As people began trading in Powell, the businesses in Garland declined. Many of the buildings were moved to other locations for other purposes or were just torn down. Today, there are only two working establishments in Garland: the ASI Bean Mill and the greenhouse. Both are following in the tradition of past Garland enterprises, depending on the agricultural community to succeed.

Garland's main street, at its height, was like that of any western town in the early 1900's. Buildings were constructed right next to each other on 25-foot lots. There was barely enough room to pass between them. (I21) Customers walked on wide boardwalks, under wooden awnings extending from the various businesses. On the south side of Main Street were the railroad, elevator, and corrals; the heart of Garland. North, east and west were hotels, saloons, livery stables, grocery stores, and all the assortments of business that would be found in a booming, western community. The businesses of Garland are described here in alphabetical order.

The alfalfa mill. Photo courtesy of Irma Yonts.

On the southwest side of the railroad tracks, a large alfalfa mill was built. It shipped out thousands of tons of high quality, Wyoming ground meal hay to eastern markets. The mill operated during the winter months, employing many local people and giving farmers the opportunity to make extra money. (MA&P 9) (The alfalfa mill will be discussed in further detail in Chapter 5.)

The Garland State Bank was located on the west side of Main Street. The two-story bank building opened for business on September 25, 1905, with a capital stock of $10,000 and an interest rate of 12 percent. "Bank your money with the Garland State Bank" was the slogan. It was operated by well-known, well-liked men, most of whom were from the local community. The board of directors consisted of H.J. Thompson, R.L. Preator, D.A. "Honest Dave" McCulloch, Joseph Neville, and C.B. King. H.J. Thompson, the bank president, was from Billings, Montana. He had become a millionaire in the lumber industry. *The Garland Guard* described him as "a very safe and conservative man". Known for his honor, R.L. Preator was a prosperous businessman from Basin. D.A. McCulloch, Joseph Neville, and C.B. King were all local men whom the people of Garland had come to trust. *The Guard* compliments McCulloch's safe and conservative manner and adds that "his personality will add much to the stability of the new bank." Joseph Neville was the county commissioner and was already well known for his integrity. C.B. King was cashier at the bank. Many of the residents had already had favorable dealings with him from the Garland Lumber and Hardware Company, where he had been working as a manager. *The Guard* describes King as "very kind, obliging, and accommodating," the kind of qualities it felt were required of a bank cashier. (NP1) In December of 1905, *The Garland Guard* printed the first report on the condition of the Garland State Bank.

The alfalfa mill looking north. Photo courtesy of Norman "Pete" Woods.

December 9, 1905 – Report of the condition of the Garland State Bank, at Garland, in the state of Wyoming, at close of business, November 9, 1905.

Resources
Loans and discounts	$4127.96	
Overdrafts, secured and unsecured	46.11	
County, City and School Warrants	727.45	
Banking house, Furniture, and Fixtures	2450.00	
Expenses paid	357.15	
Due from Nat'l Banks	-629.58	
Due from State Banks & Bankers	-3959.84	
Money reserve in Bank, vix:specie	607.25	
Legal Tender and Nat'l Bank Notes	-1147.00	
Fractional paper currency, nickels		
Pennies	6244.29	
Total		$14,052.96

Liabilities
Capital paid in	$10,000.00	
Undivided profits	35.87	
Individual deposits, subject to check	-3637.09	
Certificates of deposit, demand	-130.00	
Certificates of deposit, time	-250.00	4017.09
Total		$14,052.96

State of Wyoming, County of Big Horn – SS.

I C.B. King, Cashier of the above named Bank, do solemnly swear that the above statement is true to the best of my knowledge and belief.

C.B. King, Cashier, subscribed and sworn to before me this 4th day of December, 1905 – Thomas Long Notary Public. (NP1)

In 1906, the banking business was growing, and the board of directors decided to employ a book-keeper. Mr. Bishop, from Billings, moved to Garland to accept the position. *The Guard* reports that he "comes highly recommended as a man of sterling integrity and the strictest honesty." For the next 15 years, the Garland State Bank went about the business of banking. In June of 1916, a new cashier was needed, and E.S. Dobbs was hired.

There is still controversy over why the Bank of Garland failed. Some of those interviewed feel that Dobbs had a hand in it. Others believe that it was just the way the economy was at that time. On May 12, 1921, the Garland State Bank was closed. There were too many loans made that could not be

GARLAND STATE BANK

(Incorporated)

Capital 10,000.00

FULLY PAID UP.

Transacts a General Banking Business

Garland, - Wyoming.

—BOARD OF DIRECTORS—

H. J. THOMPSON, Pres.   C. B. KING, Cashier
R. L. PREATOR,   D. A. McCULLOGH,
JOSEPH H. NEVILLE,

Advertisement for the Garland State Bank, The Garland Guard, *November 25, 1905.*

recovered. The liabilities of the bank exceeded the assets by $30,000. (MA&P 9) Men like Burchel Hopkin's father, who had $800.00, and Earl Jones' father, who had $1000.00 in the bank, lost all their money when the bank closed. Herb Jones remembers that W.C. Wilkens was on the board of directors when the losses occurred. He said that Wilkens spent the rest of his life paying back his share of the bank losses. (I18) Today, the bank has been remodeled into a private residence. It sits in the same location but is now only a one-story building.

There were at least four barbers in Garland during the years of 1905 and 1906. It is doubtful that all four were in business at the same time, but it seems odd that Garland would go through four barbers in the span of two years. Maybe, like Charles E. Miller, they had problems with theft.

August 4, 1905 – Mr. Charles E. Miller, Garland's Tonsorial Artist, offers a reward of $5.00 to the party or parties who, several days ago, decamped with four of his best razors and a fine razor hone. If they will return the stolen property very promptly, [they will] receive the reward and no questions [will be] asked or answered. He knows who the party is and this is an easy way to avoid trouble. (NP1)

Barbershop closures were definitely not due to lack of advertisement. *The Garland Guard* favorably advertised for the other three barbers who tried their hand at making their businesses flourish.

January 13, 1905 – Garland again has a first-class barber in the person of Mr. J.F. Triplett, whose shop is located in the rear of the Gate City Saloon. Mr. Triplett came here, a short time ago, from Montana and has already made a host of friends. In the tonsorial arts, he ranks with the best in his profession. When in need of a fine, clean shave, an artistic haircut, or a nice shampoo, just ask for "Jack" Triplett. (NP1)

It appears that Mr. Triplett sought greener pastures within a year's space of time, according to the next entry.

January 20, 1906 – Mr. Costello, a young man from Butte, Montana, arrived here a few days ago and has opened a barber shop in the office of the Gate City Hotel. He is a first-class artist in the tonsorial line, a young man of clean habits, having an excellent reputation, and is a perfect gentleman; we hope the people will support him liberally. This is the only barber shop in Garland, and you will make no mistake by patronizing him. (NP1)

March 17, 1906 – W.H. Tolman, a first-class tonsorial artist, from Cody, has just opened a barber shop in the office of the Central Hotel, at the solicitation of the proprietor, Fred W. Reusch. The writer is personally acquainted with Mr. Tolman, and we know him to be one of the best barbers, if not the best, in this country. Go and try a shave and a haircut, and be convinced. (NP1)

Maybe money for a shave and a haircut was an expense that could not be spared when there was equipment that needed to be repaired by the local blacksmith. There were at least eight of them who set up shop in Garland over the years. T.E. Thompson and James F. Jensen were the two earliest ones. Thompson's shop was on the north end of town on the west side of Main Street while Jensen's was further north on the east side of the road. Both establishments catered mostly to the freighting business, shoeing horses and doing wagon repair, but their primary business was wheelwright work. (After traveling over the dry, dusty roads with heavy loads, many freighters found that a good blacksmith was frequently needed to shrink and reset the tires on their wagon wheels.) (MA&P9) For some reason however, by 1905, business must have slowed and Thompson may have moved on, as *The Garland Guard* refers to Jensen as the only blacksmith. By 1906, though, *The Guard* reported that Jensen was doing a favorable business and had to hire on a second blacksmith to work in the shop with him.

February 3, 1906 – If you have any blacksmithing you wish done by a first-class mechanic, you should take or send it, at once, to James F. Jensen, the Garland Blacksmith. He is one of the best mechanics in the Basin and he guarantees all his work to give satisfaction. (NP1)

William C. Smith was the next blacksmith to pursue his trade in Garland, and then by March of 1915, another blacksmith had set up shop.

March 2, 1915 – Mr. Fred Lloyd of Faster, MO, has leased the blacksmith shop. He opened up and began work Wednesday of this week. We hope that Mr. Lloyd makes a success of this work. (NP2)

Ted Lord remembered a man by the name of Ruland being the next blacksmith in Garland. Ruland's shop was north of the railroad tracks a couple of blocks on the east side of Main Street. He sold out to Charley Peterson. Gail Burke purchased the business next. (I22) Jack VanLake's father used to take his plow shears to Burke for sharpening. After a while Burke's blacksmith shop evolved into a garage. Burke had a deaf mechanic in his employ. Several of the residents remember him. According to Herb Jones, he was a good mechanic. He would put his hand on the fender to feel the vibration of the vehicle. He could diagnose the vehicle's problem just by the feel of the vibrations. (I18) He also did some welding. An errant spark is believed to have caused the blacksmith shop to burn down.

Roy Killiam's temporary blacksmith shop located in one of the old Garland hotels. Photo courtesy of Lloyd Killiam

They think he was using a cutting torch and some of the hot metal fell on some rags. Not knowing that he [the mechanic] closed up shop and went home. In the middle of the night, it went up. (I8)

Like Burke, Roy Killiam also ran a forge but it eventually evolved into an auto repair shop. It was located on the west side of Main Street, on the corner, about a block north of the railroad. It was on the opposite side of the street and a little south of Burke's. The Killiam family moved to Garland in 1925. In 1926 the new garage was finished. From the time they moved to Garland to the time when the garage was finished, Roy Killiam worked out of one of the old hotels. It was possibly the Gate City Hotel as in 1917, N.E. Wood and B.B. Wood had already renovated it to be a smithy/garage. Roy was dirty, like blacksmiths always were, and he did a little of everything. He sharpened plows, did some welding, and just about anything else a person might need done. Lloyd remembers his father telling someone that he had done everything but shoe horses, and he could do that too, but nobody had asked him to.

The garage had a filling station in front, where the gas pumps were pumped by hand. On the top of each pump was a glass ball with the number of gallons marked on it. Customers pumped the gas into that ball until it reached the desired amount of gallons. Then it flowed, by gravity, into their car. (I8) Inside the station, Mrs. Killiam had a glass case filled with candy bars, chewing gum, and cigarettes for sale as well. Later a storage room was built onto the garage. Lloyd remembers the local teachers storing their cars there in the winter and walking the rest of the way to school. Just before classes were released for the day, Lloyd's father would start the engines and the vehicles were all warmed up for them.

Alice Killiam in front of Killiam's garage and filling station.

Not only was Roy a good mechanic, but he also had a sense of humor. He was a friend of a man named Ketchum who had a garage and restaurant in Deaver. The two always joked that they should go into the garage business together. One could "Ketchum"; the other could "Killiam"! (119) After a successful run of his own, however, Killiam sold the garage to Virgil Eikenberry, and it became the grocery store on the corner.

John A. Thorpe was Garland's first butcher. He set up his meat market on the east side of Main Street across from the Mercantile. He ran his business out of the ground floor and lived upstairs. To the rear of the building, he had an ice house, filled with ice from the river. From his "scrupulously" clean shop, early residents could purchase "fresh and pure meats, fruits, sausages, lard, etc." Thorpe had, on hand, the choicest beef, veal, mutton, and pork. He also carried kettle-rendered lard made in Billings, Montana. On occasion, he would receive a consignment of specialty meats, things like fresh halibut, mincemeat and salmon.

The butchering business was difficult in Garland. Thorpe struggled throughout the spring of 1906, even threatening to close shop in February of that year.

February 17, 1906 - John A. Thorpe, our popular meat market man, has decided to quit the butcher business and turn his attention to other pursuits. He says that so long as the heaviest consumers in town continue to knock the local dealer, there is no show for a man trying to do the right thing by everybody, to continue in business any longer. Mr. Thorpe has a great deal of opposition to contend with, in the matter of working against these town knockers and has decided to let them have full way in the future, so far as he is concerned. We are sorry that he has concluded to quit, but under the circumstances, we do not blame him. Perhaps those knockers will wish they had purchased their beef from the local dealer about the time the hot weather begins. It will be different then. *The Guard* would do nothing towards having another butcher shop established here. There is no use in trying to do this as long as some people, for the sake of a few cents, persist in sending away for their meats. This thing of knocking the home dealer will always block in the way of progress and should be stopped. Boost! Don't Knock. (NP1)

In March, John must have had a change of heart because he added an air tight refrigerator to his meat market. It is unknown how much longer he held onto the venture. Fay Smith remembers her father taking a couple of pigs to town to sell to the butcher. Fay's father would purchase halibut and salmon with some of the proceeds from the sale. On occasion, if the butcher had it in stock, he would purchase shrimp or crab, but that didn't happen very often. Fay also remembers her family supplementing their meat supply by fishing. (I25)

The butcher was not a necessity in Garland, as most of the residents did their own meat cutting. Merl Fales remembers the community working together. Neighbors took turns butchering livestock. One would butcher a beef, and, when that was gone, the other would butcher a hog or something else. They didn't want too much meat cut up because it would spoil. Some of the meat was smoked in the smokehouse, if the family were lucky enough to have one, and some of the meat was salted and canned. Without refrigeration, the meat had to be preserved somehow to make it last longer, especially in the summer. (I7)

While most residents did not require the services of a professional, there are those who recall that Milton Cross and Alan Dugger did some butchering in later years. Alan was not a butcher by trade, but Jim and Ruth Hart both remember him helping their fathers with the task if they needed him to. (I13) Warren Cubbage described Milton Cross as a thin man who took his time. Warren related the following story about Mr. Cross's butchering style.

"There was a guy by the name of Buster Brown that lived in Garland. He was a big guy. He was in the shop one day, and Cross was butchering. Buster said, "You know, Milt, I could eat that faster than you can cut it." And Milt replied, "Yeh, but how long could you keep it up?" Buster said, "Well, till I starve to death." (I6)

The most surprising business in Garland was a car dealership. It began in March of 1916, with an Overland Car that was at the Garland Lumber and Hardware Company, for demonstration purposes. It was sold to George Hightower. (NP2) By 1917, Frank Splawn, of Penrose, became a salesman for Willy's Overland Cars and did a portion of his business on Garland's Main Street, no building was necessary. He would secure a car, and park it at the hitching rack. When a passing pedestrian showed more than idle curiosity, he would go into his sales pitch. If business in town was slow, he would drive his car out into the country to try his luck there. Once he sold that car, he would purchase another. He always had transportation and only dealt in cash. (MA&P 9)

There was at least one clothing store in town, though the residents don't remember much about it. It was a large building located north of the bank. Earl Jones thinks it might have been called Alabaster's Store. He remembers walking down the boardwalk and seeing mannequins, in women's dresses arranged in the windows. (I17) Vern Fales remembers that his family bought some of their clothes there. After the store went out of business, and the building was closed up, it became a place for the children to play. It was, however, eventually torn down. (I8)

Garland also had at least two different drugstores over the years. The first was run by D.V. Early, referred to as Doc Early, even though he was not a medical doctor. Early's Drugstore was located two buildings south of the Mercantile. In February of 1915, Doc Early sold his drugstore to Mr. J. Milton Cross and moved to a ranch near Manderson. (NP2) Later that year, Dr. Terwilliger set up a drugstore in the old Lee Hotel Building, but the business only lasted a short time.

The general stores and mercantile businesses were the most long lived and successful operatives in Garland. Over the years, there were three buildings that housed the stores and their owners. The Garland Mercantile was the first in line. It was started by James W. Beatty and Thomas Long in September of 1901. The building was located on the west side of Main Street. It was 50 feet wide and 200 feet long, with large windows that were perfect for window displays of gentlemen's winter wear, furniture, or any of the other numerous items sold there. It had in stock anything a rancher or homesteader might need, and if it didn't, special orders were available on demand. (MA&P 9) The Garland Mercantile, referred to as the "Big Store," advertised regularly in *The Garland Guard* where is promised new merchandise weekly.

May 5, 1905 – Advertisement – M. Born and Company – The celebrated Chicago clothers. Perfect fit guaranteed. Give us a trial order. Prices right. Garland Mercantile Company – Western Agents – Garland, Wyoming. (NP1)

May 5, 1905 – Advertisement – We handle the celebrated Kirkendal foot wear. We also carry a complete line of F.B. Mayer shoes, celebrated for their excellent wear qualities and comfort to the wearer. Call for these brands. Garland Merc. Co., Garland. (NP1)

May 12, 1905 - The Garland Merc. Co. has received a wagon load of beautiful seed potatoes from Burlington. Anyone wishing seed potatoes will do well to rush in their orders. $1.50 per 100 [pounds]. (NP1)

May 12, 1905 – The Garland Merc. Co. this week received a car load of flour and half a car of furniture. It is astonishing what an amount of business is done at the "Big Store" at this point. (NP1)

July 21, 1905 – Advertisement – The Big Store has just received a magnificent line of jewelry, manufactured and guaranteed by the Moline Jewelry Co., of Moline, Ill. This stock includes the finest line of finger rings, scarf pins, broaches, watch chains, charms, and lockets for both ladies and gentlemen's wear. The swellest of high grade, low-priced jewelry. – Gentlemen: If you think anything of your best girl, you can't afford to miss seeing this beautiful display and seeing is to buy. – Young Ladies: If you want to coax your best "feller" into hastening the marriage proposal, you can't do it easier than by getting him one of those elegant gold rings – He'll give it back to you on your wedding day. Garland Merc. Co. Garland Wyoming. (NP1)

"The Big Store" advertisement found in The Garland Guard, November 11, 1905

The Garland Mercantile had sales each May to clear out its winter stock, with 15 percent off winter underwear, overshirts, caps, and anything else in winter wear. By July, there were clearance sales on summer stock to make room for winter goods again. They also kept the shelves filled with groceries and cooking supplies. There was a complete line of crockery, Queen Anne Glassware, Mason fruit jars, and enamel cookware. If the young women of Garland were not lured in by the products sold at the store, they may have been drawn in by the salesmen.

October 21, 1905 – Leo Neville has accepted a position with the Garland Merc. Company's store as salesman. Leo is a pleasant, obliging and accommodating young man, and, like Carl Long is a general favorite with the girls, and between the two of them, with Mr. Beatty as a good third, there is no longer any question as to where the "sweet young things" will do their shopping. (NP1)

As Christmas approached, the "Big Store" began an advertising campaign to get the residents to do their shopping in Garland.

December 9, 1905 – The Garland Merc. Co. has received and placed on exhibit a beautiful assortment of holiday goods for old and young. And if you want the pick of the lot, you'll have to hurry. (NP1)

December 23, 1905 – The Garland Mercantile Company has just received a magnificent line of Fancy Boxed Xmas Candies. You'll have to move lively if you want your share. Nicest thing to give your best girl. (NP1)

The Garland Mercantile Company advertisement found in The Garland Guard, November 25, 1905.

In June of 1914, Mr. Carlson became the manager of the Garland Mercantile. By January of 1915, *The Powell Tribune* was reporting that the stock of goods at the store was invoiced, and manager Carlson was waiting for his replacement.

The Garland Mercantile was the first of its kind, but in March of 1906, Mr. A. Jones started a general merchandise and dry goods store. This gave the Garland Mercantile a run for its money. The Jones family moved to Garland from Hildreth, Nebraska where Mr. Jones had been a prosperous merchant. They purchased the Brown building, on the north end of town and proceeded to renovate it into a store with a stock of general merchandise. Included in his wares Mr. Jones had numerous musical instruments; most impressive among them were several fine accordions.

April 21, 1906 – A. Jones, Garland's new merchant, mention of whom we made last week, has opened up for business in the Brown Building, with a stock of general merchandise, boots, and shoes, etc. He has not entirely finished unpacking yet but will have his stock all on the shelves in a few days and has a large consignment of new goods on the way in. He has a supply of fresh cornmeal, just from the mill, which he desires to close out cheap. Mr. Jones is a fine old gentleman and comes here highly recommended. We bespeak for him a good share of the public's trade and wish him unbounded success. (NP1)

Mr. Jones did not run numerous flashy ads as the "Big Store" did. He only ran advertisements in the paper when he received a new shipment of oranges, lemons, women's dresses, shoes, or other items of interest. His store hours may have given him an advantage. He was a Seventh Day Adventist, so the store was closed from sundown Friday night until sun down Saturday night. It was open all day on Sunday. He found that this was good for business. Not only did his fellow parishioners trade on Sunday, but other residents found it advantageous to shop on Sundays as well. (MA&P9)

The railroad company's commissary may have provided whatever was lacking at Jones's store or at the Garland Mercantile, but it is only briefly mentioned in 1905 in *The Garland Guard*. It was located west of the lumber company's warehouse and advertised that is sold everything from toothpicks to locomotives. It was reported that the railroad planned to build a large barn that would hold up to 50 head of horses. (NP1) As grandiose as this sounds, the commissary must not have done the business it had hoped to, and disappeared. Nothing more was said about it.

Walter Sanders was the next person to own the Garland Mercantile Company. Earl Jones remembers trying on and buying shoes from him. Mr. Sanders would push the toe down to make sure the shoes fit. This left a lasting imprint in the leather. Earl was always "ticked off" at him for ruining his new shoes. (I17) Bonnie Hiller recalls that the Sanders were very generous people. One Christmas they gave

...A. JONES...

DEALER IN

General Merchandise

A SHOE

Like this one or like the one you want if this isn't it can be found at Jones' He is doing a big shoe business these days. His long experience in the mercantile business enables him to buy right and if a man buys right he can sell right

Remember:

Jones Pays the Freight

An advertisement for Mr. Jones's general merchandise store found in The Garland Guard, *July 7, 1906*

Bonnie an Iron Duke Wagon and her sister Beth a kiddy car. She also remembers that in one of the store's promotions, her mother won a big set of dishes with a peacock pattern on it. (I15) (They probably outlasted the Sanders years at the Mercantile.) When Walter was ready to move on, he sold the store to Joe Bob Cubbage.

Most of the residents today remember Joe Bob as the owner of the Garland Mercantile. Everyone says it was a big store with just about everything anyone would need in it. Joe Bob and his wife lived in the back of the second story. (I6) Jack VanLake remembered the fancy dinner parties Joe Bob and his wife gave. He also remembered that Joe Bob had bunions on his feet. Whenever Joe Bob got a new pair of shoes, he would cut a piece out of each one so that his bunions could stick out. (I26) Earl Jones's mother worked for Joe Bob. He used to sell bananas that were hung in big bunches over the counter. It was Earl's mother's job to cut the bananas for the customers and to grind the coffee. Melvin Scott remembers Joe Bob and the store in this way:

"I thought it was big then, but it probably wasn't. I was awful little. He used to cut a little piece off a slab of chocolate to give to the kids. [Which is why] we loved to stop there. You could [even] get kerosene there for your lamps. There was a kerosene can with a spout on it and a potato for a cork. I don't recall, but he [Joe Bob] may have had overalls and a few clothes in the store, as well. I think he did, but just basically [I remember] gloves. (I24)

Joe Bob Cubbage in the Garland Mercantile. Photo courtesy of Warren Cubbage.

While Joe Bob had the store, he became postmaster so a small part of the building was set aside as a post office. Later, the postal service provided larger quarters for him to use. He then sold the store to Jack Lewis.

Jack and his wife ran the store for a while. Ethel Heimer remembers that they did a very good job and that they tried to please everyone by taking special orders, when needed. (I14) Burchell Hopkin remembers his father purchasing groceries at Lewis's for his family and for their hired hands as well. The mercantile eventually went out of business, however, and the building was torn down.

That old store had been a source of supplies for the Garland residents, but for Bonnie Hiller it came to be just a bit more. Bonnie had gone away to nursing school but had fallen ill and had had to drop out, so she was home in the summer of 1937. One day she and her mother went to the store to sell eggs. Her mother had a crate filled with 12 dozen of them. Bonnie got out of the truck to lift the crate. Loren was sitting on the wooden steps outside the store and he jumped up to carry the eggs into the store for her. It was love, at first sight - sort of. (They had met before, but Bonnie hadn't remembered.) They were together for the rest of the summer. Then they were forced to correspond back and forth while Bonnie was in nursing school and Loren was in the Navy during the war. In 1945, Loren became Bonnie's husband. For the rest of his life, he could describe the dress Bonnie was wearing the day he came to her assistance at the store. (I15)

Garland businesses including the grain elevator and the Central Hotel. Photo courtesy of Fred Lang.

In addition to the old Mercantile Store, there was a "corner store" that catered to the needs of Garland residents. It was originally the Killam garage; then Killam sold it to Virgil Eikenberry, whose son-in-law Henry Lynn, took it over. Henry and his wife ran the store and also the garage for a while.

The grain elevator was located on the north side of the railroad tracks, east of the depot. It was owned by Peter's Milling Company and operated by Eugene McDermit. It was built to benefit those growing a surplus of grain, but it wasn't ever a working proposition. There was never enough grain coming in to justify having an elevator. (I27) Earl Jones remembers watching the elevator burn down in about 1926 or '28. (I17) The grain in the elevator at that time was a little too green and with the heat of the day, it spontaneously combusted. The elevator burned like a big candle and smoldered for two or more weeks afterwards. (I19)

When asked about the early businesses in Garland, long-time residents said that there were both hotels and saloons, but the recollections do not agree on the exact number of each. The reason may be that the owners changed so often. According to research there were, at one time, four hotels in Garland. By 1906, all of them were overflowing with guests. The Gate City Hotel came first. It was built in 1903 by C.A. Sarver at a cost of $3000 and had 17 well-furnished guest rooms. It was located on the south side of the Mercantile, so that it would be closer to the depot. The hotel catered to first-class travelers with room rates set at $2 per day. In 1904, D.A. (Dave) McCulloch became a partner, and together he and Sarver ran the livery, the saloon and the hotel. In May of 1905, however, there were changes which caused the hotel to be vacant for two weeks:

May 19, 1905 – The Gate City Hotel opened yesterday morning under new management, after a two week suspension. The new proprietor, Mr. F.W. Reusch, who has, for the past year, been doing cooking at the Government camp up in the canyon above Cody, has leased the hotel. Mr. Reusch is a first-class cook, and though a young man, he has had many years of experience, both with hotels and restaurants. His wife and children arrived from Cody yesterday morning, and they will make Garland their home, if business [allows] them [to do] so. Mr. Reusch is one of the best culinary experts in the country, and we predict for him a prosperous business in his chosen vocation here. He can handle any number of people that can conveniently crowd into the hotel, at this point. He proposes, first of all, to put up the best of fare that money can buy, and second, to treat everyone with utmost courtesy. Give the gentleman a trial, and be convinced. (NP1)

By July, the hotel was again vacant, and Sarver and McCulloch divided the property of their partnership. McCulloch received the saloon and the livery stables, while Sarver took possession of the hotel, which by September was again up and running, temporarily, as a rooming house. In October, Sarver sold it to George Shoemaker, from Germania, who had a much larger vision for the establishment.

October 28, 1905 – *Hotel Now Open for Business*
The Guard man, yesterday morning, called on George Shoemaker, who recently purchased the Gate City Hotel, and, from him, learned that the hotel is now ready for business, a first-class cook having arrived last night from Victoria, B.C.; (he has the reputation of being one of the best culinary experts of the west.) The hotel has been thoroughly renovated and made comfortable, and, in the way of edibles, the best that money can buy and good cooking can prepare, will be provided.

Mr. Shoemaker, in connection with the hotel, has leased the Frasure barn where he will be prepared to feed and properly care for teams as they come in from various points in the Basin. *The Guard* wishes the new hotel success, which it will undoubtedly enjoy. (NP1)

Sadly, Mr. Shoemaker passed away on December 10th of the same year, and Mrs. Shoemaker was unable to continue the business so the hotel changed hands once more, returning to the capable hands of Mr. Reusch. He ran the hotel, providing good food and first-class service to his patrons. In January of 1906, he was charging $5.25 for a meal ticket, and by February, he was catering to and housing homeseekers who had started coming to Garland.

February 10, 1906 – Has Good, Sure Thing – F.W. Reusch, proprietor of the Gate City Hotel, apparently has a corner on this summer's home seekers that will come in over the Burlington. He received word early this week to meet and care for the first party which arrived here Thursday, and he was right on the dot, as usual. He will have all the homeseekers to care for during the season, and if any one deserves success, it is Fred Reusch. (NP1)

The last reference to the Gate City Hotel is in June of 1906. *The Garland Guard* reported that Mr. Young of Cody was applying a new coat of roof paint to the hotel. (NP1)

Opening in October of 1905, under the ownership of E.A. Kelly, the Central Hotel had several owners as well. (It was a two-story building located opposite the depot.) In April of the following year, John Lowe of Cody took control of the hotel and promised to "conduct the place in the same orderly and conservative manner that has characterized its management under Fred Reusch." (Apparently Reusch was managing both the Gate City and the Central for a short time.) In July of 1914 Mr. and

GARLAND HOTEL

MRS. JOHN HOPKINS, PROPRIETRESS.

First Class Eating House.
First-Class Rooming House
Rates Very Reasonable · · ·

BOARD BY THE DAY, WEEK OR MONTH.
Feed Stable in Connection.

For Best Accommodations Try
The Gate City Hotel

F. W. REUSCH, Proprietor

RATES REASONABLE
EVERYTHING FIRST-
CLASS

Commercialmen's Headquarters.

Garland Wyoming

An advertisement for The Garland Hotel, also known as The Hopkin Hotel, found in The Garland Guard, *November 4, 1905.*

Gate City Hotel advertisement found in The Garland Guard, *January 6, 1906*

Mrs. Lampman moved to Garland and reopened the Central Hotel. (It had been closed for a time, it seems.) They renovated it and advertised in *The Powell Tribune* that the facility was an "up-to-date" hotel. Almost a year later, the Lampmans too gave up the effort. (Mr. Lampman was of ill health and was not getting around well.) Over the next couple years, the Central Hotel became a boarding house. Walter Best ran it until January of 1916. Then, A.S. and Jesse Johnson took over until March of 1916 when W.H. Rowley and his family rented the hotel and moved in. Finally, in December of 1917, the last proprietor, Mr. Daughters of Elk Basin, reopened the facility and established a pool hall in the Building. (NP2)

On New Year's Day, in 1902, John and Mary Hopkins arrived in Garland. John was there to locate a coal mine. In 1903, Mary purchased a town lot from the Lincoln Land Company. By 1905, *The Garland Guard* was reporting the renovation and new paint Mary Hopkin had just added to her two-story Garland Hotel, also referred to as the Hopkin Hotel. Mary was known for the delicious and tasty meals she served to her patrons.

The Hopkin Hotel clients consisted mostly of freighters from Burlington, Otto, Worland, and Thermopolis. They came to the railhead in Garland to pick up freight by means of wagon train and took it to points south of Garland. Burchell Hopkin thought the hotel consisted of eight rooms per story. Some of the ground floor was put aside for family quarters. All together there were probably ten guest rooms, well-maintained by the young Hopkin women. (I6) Each room had a fancy wash bowl and was stylishly decorated. In the reception area was a leather-bound guest register for guests to sign when they walked into the building. (I25)

In 1908, Mary moved to Penrose where she built a house and corrals and offered the occasional traveler evening accommodations. (MA&P9) In 1927, the family tore down the Hopkin Hotel and used some of the materials to build a new house. Burchel Hopkin still remembers that the bedroom doors in the new house had old hotel numbers on them. (I16)

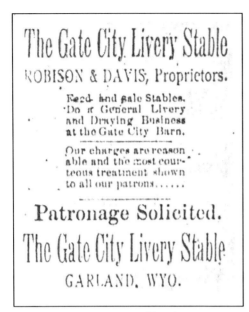

The Gate City Livery Stable advertisement as printed in The Garland Guard, *January 6, 1906.*

At the same time the hotels were bustling with business, so were the livery stables. There were two in Garland: The Gate City Livery and the Hopkin Livery. Both were operated in connection with the hotels and, at times, leased by the same people.

The Gate City Livery was run by the partnership of McCulloch and Sarver. It offered "First class conveyances and drivers [that] are furnished to all parts of the Basin at prices consistent with good transportation facilities. Horses and cattle are fed at reasonable rates by the day, week, or month." (MA&P 9) Along with transportation services and boarding rates, the Gate City Livery also sold wagons, buggies, harnesses, and saddles. After an auspicious beginning in July of 1905, McCulloch and Sarver leased Gate City livery to Rulin Robison and Charley Davis. (Robison also had the Hopkin Livery Lease that same year.)

July 7, 1905 – Rulin Robison and Charley Davis have leased the Gate City Livery barn from Sarver and McCulloch and will hereafter conduct the same on the safe and conservative system that was characteristic of the former management. They will carry on a general livery, feed and sale business. *The Guard* wishes them the highest degree of success, and as both of these young men are naturally great hustlers, they are bound to achieve it. (NP1)

In 1905, the McCulloch/Sarver partnership was dissolved, and McCulloch became full owner of the livery business. Davis and Robison continued to lease it from him. The year started slowly for them, but it began to pick up throughout the summer and the fall. The men were known for their good service and were busy taking in homeseekers and travelers all over the Basin for the rest of the year.

In December of 1905, the Gate City Livery and Stables were sold to George Lefond of Cody. Charles Davis became the night clerk at the Gate City Saloon, and Rulin Robison continued his livery business from the Hopkin Livery. Lefond began renovating as soon as he took possession. His goal was to carry on a first-class, up-to-date livery and feed business.

January 13, 1906 – The Gate City Livery Stables – Wednesday morning the writer took a stroll down to the Gate City Livery Stables, and the proprietor, Mr. George Lefond, lost no time in showing us the innumerable, substantial improvements he has made since assuming charge. We were astonished to see the amount of work Mr. Lefond has done. He has now stable room for 72 head of horses and corral room for nearly 100 more. He has several bunkhouses for the comfort of the freighters, has made a complete overhauling of the whole establishment, and is now prepared to give his patrons the best of everything in the livery business. (NP1)

By February Robison had to find a new job, as the livery firm of Schwoob and Reynolds from Cody began leasing the Hopkin Livery. They, too, added improvements to the service.

February 19, 1906 – Advertisement – Look here, Mr. Traveler – Schwoob and Reynolds – The Livery Men - wish to announce to the public of Big Horn County, that they are prepared to accommodate travelers, home-seekers, and tourists with four-horse coach or saddle horse conveniences, and coaches, with or without drivers, to all parts of the Basin at reasonable charges. – Located just east of the Hopkin Hotel – Schwoob and Reynolds, proprietors, Garland, Wyo. (NP1)

The Schwoob and Reynolds advertisement as printed in The Garland Guard, *March 10, 1906.*

In April of 1906, Dave McCulloch repurchased the Gate City Livery. He then leased it to the firm of Schwoob and Reynolds, who were already running the Hopkin Livery. Fred Reynolds was in charge of business at both.

In later years, the use of the livery changed. It became a stable where the local people could board their horses while they were building their own barns and corrals or a place for them to store hay. (I27) It also offered secret niches in which the children of Garland could play. (I1)

The Garland Lumber and Hardware Company was established in 1901. It was built on the west side of town, near the railroad tracks, north of the alfalfa mill and was a branch of the lumber company run by H.J. Thompson from Billings. (Thompson would later become one of the instigators of the Garland State Bank.) Garland Lumber and Hardware was managed by C.L. Hogle until May of 1904 when C.B. King took over. It carried a full line of hardware and boasted a very large stock of lumber, shingles, and other building materials. As a distributor for The

The Garland Lumber and Hardware advertistment as printed in The Garland Guard, *December 9, 1905.*

Continental Oil Company station in Big Horn County, they also had on hand five-gallon tin cans of kerosene and coal oil for illuminating purposes, axle grease, and other lubricants. Later, they added wagons and McCormick machinery to the stock. (MA&P 9)

In October of 1905, Garland Lumber and Hardware Company received the contract to furnish Western Construction Company with 400,000 feet of lumber to be used near Corbett for government work. The lumber supplied was for construction of bunk and lodging houses for the 50 men who were employed at Corbett. In February of 1906, the company was again awarded another contract from the government for additional work at Corbett. They constructed 33 1/2 running miles of piping that was used to build the Corbett Tunnel. The purpose was to pump out the smoke made from the rock blasting. The material used was common stove pipe, and it took 33 ten-hour days and three carloads of it to complete the job. (NP1)

Hoping to bring in the local dollars as well as the big company contracts, Garland Lumber and Hardware, just like the "Big Store," did a lot of advertising.

July 7, 1906 – Advertisement – National stoves and ranges. Awarded Gold Medal, World's Fair - 1904. If you want to get all the good out of a stove, get one that has all the good in it. The name is National. We sell them at prices that are right. We also sell McCormick mowers, rakes, binders and twine.

Our lumber and hardware business has increased to such an extent that we have been obliged to double our working force during the past few months. We attribute the increase to our policy of correct prices, courteous treatment, and the ability to handle all orders, whether large or small, with promptness. No order is too large for our capacity and none too small for our consideration. Garland Lumber and H'dware Co., C.B. King, Manager. Garland Wyoming (NP1)

Pete Wood recalled being in the hardware store in the winter when the stoves were being sold. He remembered that people would come in to talk and loaf around the nice, warm fire. One time, the manager, Les Scott, put a flashlight with orange cellophane paper around it inside a stove, making it look like fire. People backed up to the stove thinking there was a fire going. Then, they realized their mistake and started looking around to make sure no had seen them. Pete also remembered Les gluing quarters and dimes to the underside of the glass counter and then watching as people tried to pick them up. (I27) Les, apparently was quite a prankster.

From 1915 to 1917, the Garland Lumber and Hardware Company saw more changes. In January of 1915, C.B. King resigned as company manager. In October of that year, a gas station was installed on the premises. The following June (of 1916) a machine shed was constructed for farm equipment and the occasional car.

December 14, 1917 – Advertisement – Farm Implements – Now is the time to get your farm tools for the coming season. The price is not going to be so much the question, but the trouble is going to be to get them at any price, as the supply will be limited. – All implement manufactures are trying to supply the demand but do want to have anymore on hand than will be needed. – The Garland Lumber Co. – has a good stock of Oliver Two-Way and Tractor plows, Aspen

Wall potato planters, disc and spring-tooth harrows, Black Hawk manure spreaders, Titan 10-20 tractors. Come and see us. Garland Lumber Co., W.B. Thomson. Mgr.

In later years, Garland Lumber and Hardware became Longly/Templeton Lumber. W.A. Longly purchased the lumber company, and it became a branch store for Longly/Templeton in Powell. Melvin Evans was the manager for both. (I22)

In addition to all the hoteliers and hardware, lumber, and livery companies, there was also a milkman in Garland for a short time. He had about 15 customers along his route. Not only did he deliver milk to residents, but if they wanted an early morning snack along with their milk, he also sold them donuts and other pastries. Eventually, however, he decided to go into the antique business instead, so Garland no longer had a milkman. (I22)

Mrs. Elvira Lampman ran a millinery store, or hattery, out of her home, one block west of the

Mrs. Elvira Lampman's spring and summer advertisement, inviting patrons into her new store, was printed in The Garland Guard *on May 5, 1906.*

Mercantile. Stylish hats in all sizes and for all occasions, were available for men and children, as well as for the ladies. Her ample stock of trimmings included flowers, ribbons, veiling, and feathers which she used with both abundance and flair. Elvira's prices were reasonable, and she advertised that there was "no trashy stuff and nothing shoddy" in her millinery.

November 11, 1905 – Advertisement – New Stock Has Arrived – My fall and winter stock of millinery consists of – Ladies, men's, and children's hats, caps and fascinators, etc., has arrived and is now ready for inspection. My line of hat trimmings, veiling, feathers, and ribbons is complete, and I invite your inspection of these goods and my prices before purchasing elsewhere. Latest styles and best quality goods. Mrs. Elvira Lampman, Garland, Wyo. (NP1)

March 10, 1906 – Advertisement – Millinery – Man! Attention! – Don't you see that your wife's bonnet is old and shabby? You can't resist buying her a new one if you call at Grandma Lampman's and see those exquisite new styles and up-to-date creations. It's up to you to see that your wife has the best. Get Busy. Mrs. Elvira Lampman, Garland, Wyo. (NP1)

In 1906, Mrs. Lampman had a new building built on the north side of her home. In April, it was opened and stocked to the brim with the latest in spring and summer styles.

Without the newspaper, Mrs. Lampman, the Garland Lumber and Hardware Company, and the Big Store wouldn't have had anywhere to advertise, and the people of Garland wouldn't have been as well informed about what was going on in the community around them. *The Garland Guard* ran for eight years. (B9) Mr. Beatty started the newspaper. The print shop was located north of the Mercantile, and the first paper was published on September 29, 1901. Emil Vaterlaus was the editor for several years. (MA&P 9) *The Guard* charged $2.00 per year for a subscription. It accepted wood, butter, coal, and other items in trade for subscriptions. Still, Emil and his wife had problems with delinquent payments. This caused difficulty in purchasing materials to get the paper out. So, much to their disappointment every year they had to close out the subscriptions that were delinquent after they gave residents plenty of warning to get their subscriptions paid in full.

June 23, 1905 – *The Guard* is in need of money with which to send for more paper, and we are therefore under the painful necessity of asking our delinquent subscribers to "dig up." We cannot stand the paper man off with jawbone; cash MUST accompany all orders. (NP1)

In August of 1905, *The Guard* enlarged its weekly paper to an eight-page spread and began a subscription drive to try to entice residents to go out and recruit subscribers.

September 15, 1905 – Advertisement – Announcement! *The Guard* will give away, to the person sending in the largest list of new, cash, paid in advance subscribers, between October 1, 1905, and January 1, 1906, one beautiful "New Home", high arm, drop head, sewing machine, valued at $55.00. This machine is supplied with all the latest improved attachments and carries with it the manufacturers 25 year guarantee. This contest is open from Oct. 1 to Jan. 1. The minimum list brought in must include no less than 25 subscribers at $2.00 per annum, and cash must accompany all orders. This is a strictly cash proposition, and nothing else will be considered.

To the person sending in, under the same conditions, the second largest list of subscribers, we'll give a new double barrel Stevens shotgun, valued at $20.00. This contest is open to all. Gifts [will be] awarded on January 1, 1906. This is a legitimate, bonafide offer and is worth trying for. Address all communications to *The Guard*, Garland, Wyoming. Receipts [will be] promptly issued from this office. (NP1)

Besides subscriptions, *The Guard* made money selling advertisements and printing up stationery, letterheads, noteheads, billheads, statement heads, and envelopes. Several businesses took advantage of the offerings, and *The Guard* was really able to show off its printing skills in addition to its advertising. (Several of these have been reprinted here.)

October 14, 1905 – Advertisement – *The Garland Guard* – Published at the "Gateway" of the Big Horn County – The People's Advocate – Entered at Garland, Wyoming, Post Office as second class mail matter – Emil Vaterlaus and Rose Vaterlaus – Publishers – Advertising rates: legal rates charged for legal advertising. Reading advertising locals - 10 cents per line, first insertion; 5 cents per line, each subsequent insertion

Display advertising – Double column, per inch, per month ……. $1.00
Single column, per inch, per month ………. $ .50

Special rates on advertising contracts [are] made for the whole year. Matters for insertion this week must be in the hands of the printer no later than Thursday morning. (NP1)

In June of 1906, George Phipps began leasing *The Garland Guard*. He was a well-known newspaper man, and *The Cody Enterprise* stated that he would, "no doubt, make *The Guard* one of the leading newspapers in the Basin." He didn't waste any time working toward that prediction. He enlarged the paper to a seven-column folio, instead of six columns. He started getting more advertisers from Cody. He also hired Frank Bennet from Cody as a printer. (NP1) However, despite all the improvements *The Guard* closed in 1907 when Emil Vaterlaus moved it to Cowley to start *The Cowley Progress*. (MA&P 9)

 In 1910, Bert C. Peterson took his shot at the newspaper business. He started *The Garland Courier* in the same building where *The Garland Guard* had been housed. *The Courier* remained in Garland for five years until Peterson moved it to Powell and renamed it *The Powell Courier*. (MA&P 9) About that time, *The Powell Tribune* was running a section in its paper entitled "Garland News."

Getting the newspaper out wouldn't have been possible without the post office. On November 5, 1901 the Garland Post Office officially opened. It was first located in the Mercantile Store, about halfway through the building, on the north side. James W. Beatty was the postmaster. The office was the distribution center for all the mail in the eastern and southern part of the Basin. The mail came in on the train, was taken to the post office, and was sorted. Then the carrier took it to the proper location, picked up the mail, and brought it back to Garland where it too could be sorted and put on the train. Garland remained the distribution point until 1906. (MA&P 9)

Early in the 20th century, the Strong family, from Lovell, had three government-contracted mail routes that they covered by horse and buggy. Bessie and Edna Strong were the young women who often carried the mail to Kane, to Crooked Creek, to the Dryhead, to Garland, to the Mason/Lovell Ranch, and to Ewing, Montana. From 1903 to 1906, Bessie had the Garland route. She left the post office in Lovell and rode to the Dryhead, then to the Mason/Lovell ranch, and finally to Garland. She had from 7:00 am to 7:00 pm to complete this run. Edna and the girls' father, Frank, ran the other two routes. Since the Strong girls, on their own merit, were known to be good shots, everyone left them alone when they were carrying the mail. (B1)

Some of the mail was contracted out to carriers and some of it was delivered by the stagecoach. In 1905, Ora Allen operated the stage-

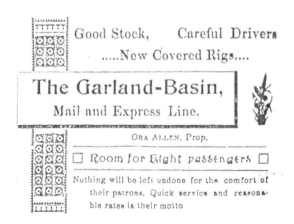

Ora Allen's stageline and mail services were advertised in The Garland Guard *on November 4, 1905.*

VOL. V, NO. 35   Garland, Big Horn County, Wyoming, Saturday, June 2 1906. $2.00 Per Annum

....A. JONES....

General Merchandise

Having opened up a small stock of goods in the Brown Building, I desire to say to the trading public that I will sell goods as cheap as can be done with sound business principle, and by honest dealing I wish to merit a share of the trade.

The store will be closed from sun down Friday night until sun down Saturday night and open all day Sundays.

Yours very respectfully,

A. Jones.

Remember:

Jones Pays the Freight

LOOK HERE MR. TRAVELER

Schwoob & Reynolds,

The Livery Men, wish to announce to the public of Big Horn county, that they are prepared to accommodate travelers, homeseekers and tourists with four-horse coach or saddle horse conveyances, coaches with or without drivers, to all parts of the basin at reasonable charges.

Located Just East of Hopkin Hotel

Schwoob & Reynolds, Proprietors, Garland Wyo.

Coutant & Jones

— Dealers in —

Irrigated Farms in the celebrated Grey Bull Valley at from $7.00 to $25.00 per acre. We have just what you want.

— Write us at —

Burlington, Wyoming.

PROFESSIONAL

JOSEPH H. McVILLE,

Surveyor and U.S. Commissioner

BYRON,   WYOMING.

M. CHAMBERLIN
DENTIST
Cody - - - Wyo.

Wm. Blackburn
NOTARY PUBLIC

H. S. RIDGLEY
LAWYER
Will Practice in All Courts
BASIN.   WYO.

Geo. B. TAYLOR
ENGINEER
— AND —
ARCHITECT
CODY   WYO

The Gate City

GARLAND is situated on the branch of the Burlington Railway which taps the Big Horn Basin. It lies in the heart of the Shoshoni project of the Reclamation Service.

The Big Horn Basin

is the coming section of the West.

WE BOW

With this issue the editorial and business management of The Guard is assumed by Geo. A. Phipps.

Good Words

Dr. Powell's Ashes At Rest

F. J. HISCOCK

The Leading Photographer

High Grade Studio Work At Reasonable Prices. Best Collection of Mountain Views and Park Scenery to be Seen Anywhere. Full Stock of AMATEUR PHOTO SUPPLIES. Mail Orders Promptly Filled.

IT WILL COST YOU NOTHING TO CALL WHEN IN CODY

You Can Get It At CAMPBELLS

We wish to announce to the people of Garland and vicinity that we carry a complete stock of Drugs and Druggist's Sundries. We are prepared to fill your wants at the lowest prices.

We will look after your mail orders the same as if you were at our store, in person selecting your own goods and give it our prompt attention.

Campbell Drug Co.

Successors to A. L. CUMMINGS

Cody - - - Wyo.

MATCH MAKER

R. E. Naylor

Veterinary Surgeon ::

CODY STEAM LAUNDRY,

LEGALS

Notice to Stockholders.

Notice to Stockholders.

The front page of The Garland Guard. *June 2, 1906.*

line to Basin. He carried the mail and up to eight passengers in one of two elegant stagecoaches. While Mr. Allen advertised quick service, *The Garland Guard* reported that the mail was often late and undependable. In October, O.C. Morgan took over Allen's contract and began running the mail and stage between Basin and Garland as well as between Frannie and Worland.

In 1906, the mail contracts were up again for the routes from Garland to Lovell and from Garland to Basin. Fred Reusch and William West decided to apply for the opportunity.

June 30, 1906 – Awarded Contracts

The post office department has awarded the mail contract for mail between Garland, Byron, Cowley, and Lovell to William West. This contract calls for mail six times per week. For this, they will pay $1200 per year. The former price was $912.

The contract for carrying the mail between Garland, Penrose, Germania, Basin, and Burlington was awarded to Fred Reusch. The former price was $2143.68, and the contractor now gets $3000.

The new contractors will start their services as soon as possible, probably by July 1st. These gentlemen are capable men and will handle the stageline in a satisfactory manner to the government and to the public; we can be assured of two good stagelines from Garland. (NP1)

The post office was housed in many different locations, first in the depot, later in the Mercantile, and then in the drug store, in 1910. Luther Wood constructed a building on the east side of Main Street in 1912, and ran the post office from there, with help from his daughter, Ethel. (NA 1) In 1916

Joe Bob Cubbage and some Garland children putting up the flag at the post office. Photo courtesy of The Homesteader Museum.

A.B. Campbell moved the post office again, this time to the Lee Hotel Building where Thura Campbell assisted in its operation. Finally, the telephone office was turned into a post office, and Joe Bob Cubbage became the postmaster. The new post office building was very small, and narrow, and inside that, there was a partition. The front section was tiny, with barely enough room to turn around. It hosted a row of mail boxes. The partition had a window in it, behind which was the postmaster. (I8) Pete Wood remembers Joe Bob taking his two-wheeled cart to the train in the morning to get the mail. He would then bring it back and sort it in the back room. Later in the afternoon, he would return the mail, in the cart, to the train. (I27)

The following is a list of the Garland postmasters from 1901 to 1972:

James W. Beatty	November 5, 1901
Mrs. Vinnie R. Naylor	January 23, 1910
Luther J. Wood	October 26, 1912
Arthur B. Campbell	February 24, 1915
Mrs. Mary J. Murray	September 22, 1917
Albert O. Crane	August 29, 1918
J.B. Cubbage	April 1, 1935
Mrs. Eliza Basham	March 31, 1950
Marsden A. Christoffersen	August 1, 1951
Mrs. Gladys M. Malliot	September 18, 1952
Mary L. Malliot	December 31, 1972 (MA&P 9)

The post office was a favorite gathering place in Garland. Many of the residents fondly remember the later postmasters. Bonnie Hiller says that Joe Bob delivered Christmas packages from her sister on Christmas Eve, since he knew how much those packages meant to Bonnie. She also recalls Gladys Malliot staying open late on Christmas Eve because she expected the mail truck would come in late and that the packages it carried were ones the children were to open on Christmas morning. (I15)

Ezra Lewis was the rural mail carrier. Residents remember that he was very efficient at his job. His route included Garland, Penrose, the south side of the river to Byron, and the area running almost to Deaver and back again to Garland. Ted Lord said that Mr. Lewis needed a new car every three years because he put 40 to 50 miles on them a day. (I22) When Mr. Lewis was not available, Rance Gillison and Herb Jones were the substitute mailmen. Herb remembers that Mrs. Malliot always covered the floor with newspapers when it rained or snowed. She tried valiantly to keep the mud off the floor when the mail was carried in and out of the post office. (I18)

On March 30, 1973, the post office was discontinued in Garland and relocated in Powell. Les Lawrence was there when it closed. He was saving stamps at that time, and he wanted the last stamp from the Garland Post Office. He asked the postmistress what time she planned to close, and she told him, "Well, about 6:00." So at ten minutes to 6:00, Les and his mother-in-law went to the post office. Les had his letter in hand and he received the last cancellation stamp from the Garland Post Office, on his letter. He had his camera with him too, and, as they were leaving the building, he stopped to take a picture of his mother-in-law to commemorate the occasion. (I21) That photo can be seen on the sign in Garland that marks the location of the post office.

Just as the post office and the newspaper were important to the life of the community, the relevance of Garland's merchant and service industries should not be underplayed. In association with, and sometimes independent of the hotels, were the restaurants of the town. Mary Hopkin provided her patrons with delicious home-cooked meals, and, on occasion fed the people of the community, as well. In 1905, Ed Kelly ran a nice restaurant out of Thorpe's Meat Market. They probably worked together. John supplied the meat, while Ed prepared it for the customers. In February of 1906, a new bakery and another restaurant were added to the mix.

February 10, 1906 – Restaurant has changed hands – Mesars. Ward and Mack have just opened a restaurant and bakery in the rooms adjoining the new Lee and Horn Saloon. The place has been thoroughly renovated and repapered. The firm has a tip-to-first-class, short order, eating house and puts up hot and tasty meals. The place is open early and late for the accommodations of the belated travelers. We wish the gentlemen unbounded success. They solicit patronage of the public and guarantee satisfaction. (NP1)

According to Pete Wood, the restaurants, unfortunately, didn't stay in business for very long. Most were there primarily to take advantage of the money that could be made from the travelers coming off the railroad. When the track continued past Garland, so did the restaurant owners. Pete, however, did have one story to relate that his father had told him about one of the early, little, ramshackle restaurants in Garland.

"My dad bought a hamburger, and he said it was far from a reasonable price, which made my dad a little upset. He said, 'I'm never coming back here again to buy a hamburger.' The man running the place said, 'I don't expect you to.' (He was making hay while the sun shines.) (I27)

Like the hotels of Garland, the number of saloons recalled by the residents varied. Many thought there were anywhere from five to seven of them, but according to research there were only four. Some of them had accommodations for overnight guests, and some also served meals to their customers.

The Garland Saloon appeared first. It was built in 1901, by Brewer and Lee of Billings, on the west side of Main Street. Charles E. Birks was the manager. He kept in stock the best wines, liquors, and cigars and the celebrated Billings Brewing Company's Pilsner Beer. The saloon also sported a lunch counter which added to its popular appeal. Catering to the freighters and the construction crews that came through town, the Garland Saloon was the only local saloon until 1903. (MA&P 9)

In that year, A.C. Burke came from Oregon and built the Crystal Saloon. It was a modern structure on the east side of South Main Street near the depot. Composed of native lumber, it cost $2000 and had all the conveniences of a first-class saloon, with eight lodging rooms upstairs. (MA&P 9) At some point, the Crystal Saloon was sold to O.G. Norton, and in September of 1905, E.A. Kelly began leasing it and was considering converting it into a hotel. (NP1) This building may have become the Central Hotel, as, in October of the same year, E.A. Kelly was advertising in *The Garland Guard* that the Central Hotel was open for business.

By 1905, the Gate City Saloon, located next to the Gate City Hotel, was a thriving concern. It was operated by Sarver and McCulloch, who also were running the livery.

The Gate City Saloon advertisement as printed in The Garland Guard, *November 4, 1905.*

May 5, 1905 – Advertisement – Gate City Saloon. Sarver and McCulloch, Props. Best Whiskies, Brandies, Wines, and Cigars always on hand …. We are wholesale and retail agents for the Storz Brewing Co's. Famous Blue Ribbon Beer… All orders, from a bottle to a carload, are carefully attended to. Ask for pure barley malt when you call in … Give us a trial. Our prices are right, [located] next door to the Hotel. Garland, Wyoming (NP1)

In July of 1905, the partnership between Sarver and McCulloch was dissolved and McCulloch became full owner of the saloon. McCulloch immediately began to renovate the premises. He hired Mr. Miller to paint, Mr. Ellis of Basin to wallpaper, and Ed Kelly to do the carpentry work. By the first of August the saloon had a new floor, and fresh wallpaper, and the ceiling had a double coat of white paint that enhanced the decor.

August 11, 1905 – The Gate City Saloon is now one of the neatest and most comfortable resorts in the Basin. Everything is fixed up in the finest style. The interior is decorated with beautiful paintings, some of them the work of Miss Mary McCulloch, who is a really fine artist. The wainscoting, along the interior walls, has been repainted, the doors and window casings also have been nicely painted, and the whole interior, as well as the exterior, looks like a new building. The place is a decided credit to the enterprising proprietor, Mr. McCulloch, and to the barkeeper, Mr. Chase E. Miller, who is largely responsible for the neat appearance of the building. A large, new gasoline lamp has been added, which illumines the house as brightly as the sun at noonday. No one is more pleased with the improved appearance of the hall than Dave himself. (NP1)

Dave McCulloch continued to keep the saloon well stocked and in good order. He made sure to have on hand the best wines, liquors, cigars, and beers and gave courteous treatment to all of his patrons. He went on to make more improvements in the appearance of the saloon, as well. In October, he purchased half a dozen Congress chairs from the Garland Merc. Co. for the "solo friends and saloon bums." In January of 1906, Dave ordered a gasoline light plant for the saloon as he had been having problems with his previous lighting system. In June of the same year, he repainted the front of his saloon and later that month, the bartender, Chase Miller, purchased it from him and vowed to dispense "liquid hilarity in the fashion of up-to-date mixers." (NP1)

The Lee Saloon was one of three which, in 1906, were offering spirits to the local community. In December though, having faith that Garland would soon be one of the bigger towns in the Basin, Walt Lee of Billings contracted with Thomas Fitzsimmons to construct a two-story building for him opposite the Gate City Hotel. The upper story was made into office space for professional men, and in the lower story, was another saloon. In mid-January, the saloon was open for business.

February 10, 1906 – The Lee Saloon – The Lee Saloon, which recently began business here, and which is owned by Walt Lee and Jack Horn, has been nicely papered and decorated, on the interior, and fitted up in elaborate style. This firm has been established the rule to sell only the very best of beer, wines, liquor and cigars that can be had on the market. They handle the celebrated Budweiser and Val Blats Beers and have the celebrated Billings Brewing Company's beer on draft. Jack Horn is in charge and is a genial, good natured gentleman. Mr. and Mrs. Horn are popular, young people. (NP1)

In their hey-day, the saloons of Garland did a good business. Gambling and social gatherings were held at all of them. Because the community of Powell was dry, the saloons were among the few businesses that the people of Powell patronized in Garland. Since they were so lucrative, one wonders what caused the saloons to go out of business? In all likelihood, Prohibition was responsible. Earl Jones remembers that all the saloon buildings were closed down in the early 1920's. (I17)

Since Garland was still, for the most part, a farming, ranching community, it was no surprise to learn that it had a veterinary for a short time. In 1905, Ralph Naylor resigned his position at the Garland Lumber and Hardware Company and returned to college to continue his studies to become a veterinarian. In April of 1906, he was back, and advertising his services as a veterinary surgeon, even though he had one more year to go before he graduated.

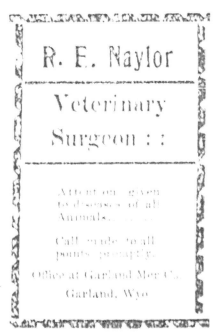

May 12, 1906 – Dr. R.E. Naylor, our efficient veterinary surgeon, has already worked up a nice practice in this and surrounding towns and has effected several remarkable cures on horses, which were considered beyond care, and in every case, he has been entirely successful, all of which shows that he thoroughly understands his business. Next year, he will graduate with the genuine prefix of full fledged V.S. (NP1)

Whenever area residents drive through the little town of Garland from now on, they might stop to consider the buildings that remain there, the vestiges of the ones that are gone, and the businesses that used to keep the town bustling. It is certain that with those thoughts in mind, they will never look at this little bend in the road in quite the same way again.

Ralph Naylor advertised his veterinary services in The Garland Guard, May 12, 1906.

Chapter 4 - Unlikely Citizens

While Garland depended on the railroad to bring people and supplies, there was another group of transients on whom the residents also came to rely. These were the hoboes and the peddlers. The peddlers brought with them goods and services that were not readily available locally, while the hoboes often exchanged hard work for a warm meal and a place to stay. Although not a permanent part of the community, these individuals were important and have earned a right to their own chapter.

Two peddlers who stood out in the memories of those individuals who were interviewed were the Watkins man and the Raleigh man. They both pulled large wagons, and later drove large trucks, filled to the brim with extracts, medicines, liniments, and other household items. Jim Hart described their wagons as "traveling drug stores." Their target market was the housewives. Once a month, the traveling stores drove from farm to farm selling their wares. Like today's Schwan's man, they made shopping more convenient. There was no more sending husbands on long trips to town with a list, hoping they would get the right thing. The Watkins and Raleigh men brought supplies right to the door.

Residents of Garland remembered a least three different Watkins Men who served the Garland area. Hubert Hart thought Jay Milton Cross may have sold Watkins products. Fred Ferh and Mr. Lions were also mentioned as Watkins salesmen. The Watkins men were known for their spices, vanilla, coffee, and other reliable products. Pete Woods remembered the Watkins man selling nuts and other goods. He often gave the kids a pack of gum and sometimes California fruit. These are fond memories that several Garland residents share from their childhood. Vern Fales tells about the Watkins man:

"Mr. Lions was the Watkins man. He sold Watkins products for a long time. He sold everything - vanilla, salt, kitchen commodities, and salves. One thing that Dad used to buy a lot of was salve for the cows' udders. They would get chapped, and that would fix them up." (I8)

The Raleigh man sold the same goods: liniment, Mentholatum, vanilla, and some cooking items. Lloyd Heimer remembers a song they sang, as kids, to get a stick of gum. Nobody had money back then, and this was how they earned a stick of gum:

"Raleigh, Raleigh, six kids in all"
"Raleigh, Raleigh, we all like gum!" (I14)

Darwin Franklin remembers the Raleigh man staying at their house at the end of the day. He would spend the whole night, clear into the next day, and then get up to continue his route.

The people of Garland began to look for these two peddlers. They broke the monotony and were great company. The children especially watched for them as both brought gum. Eventually, as transportation and roads improved, the peddlers stopped coming around. It became easier to go to town and get what was needed and people didn't need to wait around for the Watkins and Raleigh men to come anymore. (Watkins products can still be found, but no one comes to the door selling their wares these days.)

Other products were also peddled in the Garland area. There were traveling salespeople who sold instruments, auto parts, medicines, and apples.

June 9, 1906 - Frank P. Whitmore, the Kimball Piano man, is making another tour of the Basin. If you want anything in the music line, from a phonograph to a piano or pipeorgan, write him in Garland, and he will see you and save you money, by shipping direct from the factory. (NP1)

Pete Woods remembered another man who came around to tune pianos, while Lucy Cozzens tells the story of the first peddler who came walking up their long road to the house.

"We had very few people who came to the house. The first one [peddler] we got was when our daughter was still in our arms, and this guy wanted to sign her up for a musical instrument, so she would be ready for school. She was too young to know what she wanted to play, or if she would even want to play an instrument, but this guy tried selling us one anyway. (I4)

Lloyd Killiam's father at one time owned the automotive garage in Garland, and he remembers Mr. Murphy, a salesman with Northwest Auto Supply in Billings. For 30 years, Mr. Murphy sold mostly parts and garage supplies. After being on the road for several days and not having a good home-cooked meal, he often ended up at Killiam's. He had a big appetite, and Lloyd's mother always accused him of getting to the house right at supper time. Mr. Murphy not only helped supply parts for the garage but also became a good friend of the family.

 Ethel Heimer and Katie Brown, who are sisters, both recall a salesman who sold medical kits. Katie describes the medical kit as a big case with everything in it. All the items were labeled for what they were used for. There was also an assortment of pills and antiseptics. Ethel wasn't sure that they always took the right thing, but usually, whatever they chose seemed to take care of all their small medical problems.

Mr. Betts was the apple salesman. Earl Jones told the story of the day Mr. Betts wrecked his car.

Mr. Betts pulled out in front of an oil truck near our house. He drove an old 30's style car, and that car just got knocked clean off its spokes. Mr. Betts always wore a derby hat and that was the only time I can say I saw him without it. He wasn't hurt, but his hat was knocked off his head and his car was badly damaged. (I17)

Mr. Lieberman was the junk buyer, or one of the first recyclers, in the Garland area. Ethel remembers him buying copper, iron, lead, and aluminum. He also bought sheep's wool, and muskrat and coyote hides. Ethel was fairly certain he resold them in Billings for a profit.

Some of the peddlers were invited into people's home and were gladly fed, but some may have taken the hospitality of the Garland residents for granted. Herb Jones recalls a funny story in which one salesperson wasn't so welcome.

"There was one saleswoman who stopped by one night and asked to stay the night. My dad was gone, and I remember that my mother said we didn't have a room. I told Mom that I could sleep on the floor or on the spring couch, and she could have my room. The saleswoman ended up staying, and Mother said she never slept the rest of the night. (I17)

While peddlers brought with them needed supplies, the hoboes brought strong backs and helping hands. From Garland's earliest years through the Dust Bowl era, the hoboes used the railroad as their means of transportation. The residents of Garland didn't always look forward to their coming but were charitable to them and appreciated their help. Some caused trouble, but most were just looking for work, a place to sleep, and a warm meal. The following is the only bad report found. In 1905, *The Garland Guard* reported:

Constable Jensen made two very important arrests here Saturday night. Two hoboes slugged a third one, who was known to have considerable money, and robbed him of all he had. This happened in Cody, and after the robbery had been accomplished, the hoboes came to Garland and were captured by Constable Jensen. Next morning, special Deputy, B.G. Lantry and George LaFond took the happy couple to Basin, where they are to answer to the charge of highway robbery. (NP1)

The hoboes were a regular sight along the railways. Residents remember them riding flat cars through town to the hobo camp west of town, near where the railroad tracks cross the Bitter Creek. Merl and Glen Fales walked by the hobo camp one day, early in the morning. They were invited to breakfast but were a little spooked and shy, so they decided to decline the offer. During trips to Billings, Ethel remembers seeing hoboes along the tracks. She recalls their having a little railroad car hut in Laurel where they could get coffee and hamburgers. Jack VanLake remembered one man who helped with the threshing in return for a place to stay.

"My dad started threshing, and this guy came bumming around. Dad hired him. He let him sleep upstairs in the room next to me. (Mom didn't like that.) He worked hard through the threshing season for Dad." (I26)

Even though the peddlers and hoboes did not call Garland home, each one was accepted into the Garland community. Some became friends who could always count on a place to stay on their way through, and some just enjoyed the kindness given to them by the Garland residents. They became "unlikely citizens" of Garland, part of the community life, and part of its history.

Chapter 5 ~ Agriculture: Working Together

No one needs to be told that farming and ranching are hard work. The people of Garland knew this, but farms and ranches were still a draw. Many came, but some did not survive. The ones who stayed made the land bloom. They learned how to irrigate and raise livestock on it. Some years, they battled against Mother Nature, while in other years, Mother Nature was their best friend. Citizens of all ages worked together to keep crops and livestock growing, even during hard times.

To become a farmer or rancher, you first need land. In Garland's early days you either purchased property from someone who had already worked the land, or you homesteaded and did the work yourself. There were several people who came before the canal system was built, and began to homestead and clear the land. By 1905, men like Joseph H. Neville, Thomas Long, and W.S. Collins were promoting the area and trying to sell property in and around Garland with the help of *The Garland Guard.* By this point, calls were being made to Joseph Neville to make final verification of homesteads or desert entry lands, and others were calling to have their lands sold.

October 28, 1905 – Joseph H. Neville, at Garland Wyoming – Sell Land – Ranch 80 miles from Garland – 100 head of cattle, under cultivation, 240 acres, water rights, will sell on reasonable terms. (NP1)

October 28, 1905 – Thos. Long, at Garland, Wyoming – 140 [acres] under cultivation, 160 acres total, 6 miles from Lovell, water rights. Will sell on reasonable terms. (NP1)

September 1, 1905 – W.S. Collins, the hustling Big Horn Basin colonizer, returned Tuesday from an extended eastern trip, where he has been doing more missionary work for this county. Mr. Collins is another of those enterprising rustlers who is doing everything possible to colonize the Basin with a desirable class of people. Much of this year's increase in population is due to just this sort of missionary work on the part of Mr. Collins. (NP1)

October 7, 1905 – There are several rentable houses in town just now, caused by a number of our good people moving out upon their homesteads. (NP1, NWN)

Even before the farmers were preparing to bring water to the land, ranchers were learning how to profit from it. The land surrounding Garland was open range. Cowboys and sheepherders were part of the landscape. The stockyards were built on the east side of Garland, along the railroad, to transport livestock out to market. Many young Garland residents learned a thing or two about hard work by hanging around the stockyards. Merl Fales realized what he wanted to do with his life while observing the cowboys' activities there.

"When I started out, I was going to be a cowboy. That's always been my direction in life, from the beginning. We didn't want to be politically correct. We hadn't heard of such a thing. Nobody had any interest in sitting in those swivel chairs when there was work to be done." (I7)

The children of Garland were always watching the cowboys. Earl Jones tells a story that his uncle, Bud Jones, told him about the cowboys who gathered at the stockyard after long hours of work.

"Uncle Bud used to tell about going down after school to watch the cowboys come out with a tub or a big pan full of whiskey. They all sat in a circle and passed a long handled dipper around. And then, some of them would get drunk. Bud remembered, in particular, a drunk, little cowboy with a cigar who often got to arguing and would throw his cigar down over by the hitching rail, where the horse manure was. Uncle Bud said that after awhile, the little cowboy would go over, pick it up, brush it off and stick it back in his mouth. This was a pretty regular occurrence." (I17)

While cattle were probably the first livestock to roam free on the land around Garland, it wasn't long before sheep were grazing there as well. As early as the winter of 1886, Charles Worland was wintering his sheep on the range. He was headquartered south of Byron, and although he had heavy losses that horrible winter, he persevered in his endeavors. He was followed by Thomas and James Howell from Tennessee. They brought 3,100 head into the Basin in 1888. Four years later, they were joined by James's son, James F. Howell, and their herd totaled 10,000 that year. The Howells were headquartered south of Byron and ran sheep across the entire Basin, up into the mountains. R.B. (Dick) Heritage also had sheep in the area and was a neighbor of the Howells. During this time, a bridge was built at Penrose, across the Shoshone River, to benefit freighters and the herdsmen. Several bands of sheep were on the trail to Garland each year for spring shearing at the shearing corral that had been built southeast of town on Bitter Creek. (B9)

Garland soon became the headquarters for three large sheep outfits - one run by the Lampman brothers, James and Darrel - one by the Sperry brothers, and the other by Paul Richter. The Lampmans hailed from the Shell Creek area, originally coming to the Basin from Iowa in the fall of 1888. James became a Justice of the Peace and a leading citizen in the community. The Lampmans operated their venture south of Penrose. Paul Richter, also a substantial citizen, ran his sheep in the Garland area in the winter and kept them in Cody during the summer.

J.B. Sperry's unmatched team of mules was more noteworthy than were his sheep. His team was made up a brown mule and a white one, hitched to his trap wagon. One mule always traveled a step ahead of its mate. When the old man wished to increase their speed, he would apply the whip to the mule in the lead and was noticeably more energetic about it if he had made a recent stop at one of Garland's saloons. A large yellow shepherd dog always accompanied his master, riding in style in the wagon. Needless to say, Sperry was always easily recognized, whenever he came to town. (MA &P9)

In 1905, wool prices were climbing, and the flock masters of Garland were doing well. Even after the harsh winter of 1906, there were few losses of sheep reported, and the herders were "singing the praises of our own matchless winter weather." (NP1) As late as February, 1917, *The Powell Tribune* was reporting that sheep were being taken into the hills for another summer season, after wintering on hay grown in Garland. (NP2)

In later years, Merl Fales decided that he too wanted to become a flock master. His first attempt began with a sick sheep that was left in the stockyard.

"One time, they [the stockmen] brought a bunch of sheep into the stockyards. They [the herders] loaded them up and left. One of the sheep was real weak. Warren Cubbage and I doctored it up. As far as I can remember, I think it lived for quite a while. They just abandoned it." (I7)

Merl and his brother Glen learned some hard lessons about being flock masters and good neighbors:

"Glen and I would go over to our neighbor, Rance Gillison's. We were always helping him because we liked to work. We helped with his band of sheep quite often. He had three dogs. One was a Spitz. He wasn't a stock dog, but Rance left him out there at the farm. Why he had that one, I don't know. One day, the dogs got into Rance's sheep and killed a bunch of them. (That Spitz might have been the cause of it.) The dogs just wrecked the little band of sheep. All the neighbors heard about it. 'The dogs got into Gillison's sheep.' I don't remember the kind of dog we had at that time. I know we had one, but we didn't have one that chased sheep. We were sure thankful for that. Our cousin,

Glen packing Merl around the farm. Photo courtesy of Merl Fales.

Herb Wilson, who was our neighbor, had a pretty good stock dog. When he heard that dogs had gotten to Rance's sheep, there was nothing Herb could do to help Rance financially. So he called his dog and looked at his mouth. The dog had blood on his mouth. Herb went to the house, got his gun, and shot the dog. He left him lying there on the sidewalk all winter. It showed he cared. My dad always said, 'A good neighbor is worth more than another team of horses.' That was how we survived. We worked together. (I7)

"Rance helped Glen and me get our own flock started. Beside his place, Rance had a little bunch of sheep. In the summer, he trailed his sheep to the mountain; then in the fall or winter, they would come back down. One day, when they were getting ready to ship the sheep out on the railroad, they got Glen and me over there to help. There was a guy by the name of Johnson that came to ship the sheep. Rance told us Johnson would go 'real fast with these sheep.' (The ewes might have been worth $2.) We were in the barn. Johnson was out by the train. Rance told us again that Johnson was going to go through the sheep fast and that a lot of the sheep would drop out. Johnson would lose a lot of sheep. I knew what he was thinking. As the sheep dropped out, Rance was going to grab them and throw them in the barn. He was right, and as the sheep started dropping out, we would grab them. I don't know how long that went on, but I remember keeping count. Finally, Johnson got ready to go with the sheep. He left, and Rance said, 'You better take your sheep home.' That is how we got started in the sheep business. Of course, we had already been feeding bum lambs. So we already had a few sheep. Now we had quite a flock. (I7)

"Our flock was now good-sized and producing wool. The best part of this is that the market started jumping up. The government was still buying wool and making shipments from Powell. Glen and I went down there with beet seed sacks full of wool. We had Icky Wasden shear our sheep for us, and we put our wool in beet seed sacks because the wool sacks were great big. We were doing pretty good. We even pitched some dead wool, of course, you have to have a handkerchief over your nose because you just pull the wool off the sheep after she's dead and rotten. You kind of have to stay downwind from anyone for a little bit. But it paid off. We took all our dead wool and good wool. We got in line. Then this guy comes to the back of the line and asks what we were doing at the back of the line. 'You are just the men we want up front here,' he told us. He wanted us to sign up in the Wool Growers Association. It didn't cost anything. We got up to the head of the line, in front of all the guys with big buckboards full of wool. They weighed us out. They bought our dead wool, bought our good wool, paid us off, and signed us up in the Wool Growers Association. Life wasn't too bad. We had the attitude for life. The Depression was breaking, and everyone was fine." (I7)

Long before Glen and Merl became flock masters, the people of Garland were well aware that they would need more than ranching to support the population they hoped would settle in the area. They knew that, in this dry climate, water was necessary to make the land bloom with people and agriculture. *The Garland Guard* kept the citizens posted as to the progress of the Shoshone Irrigation Project, with a focus on the Garland division:

October 7, 1905 – Hyrum Cook of Cowley has been engaged to drive a team for a party of U.S. Surveyors, between Garland and Lovell. (NP1, NWN)

November 11, 1905 – We are receiving numerous inquiries from people in various parts of the country as to when the land, under the proposed Shoshone Irrigation Project, will again be open for entry, but not being on the inside, we are unable to furnish the required information. We suggest that all those wishing these questions answered, write to the Hon. Secretary of the Interior in Washington or to some of the office [staff] in the employment of the Reclamation Services. (NP1, NWN)

April 14, 1906 – *The Garland Canal – The Secretary of the Interior Advertises for Bids for Construction of Division Number One.*

Special to *The Guard* – Washington D.C., April 10. – The Secretary of the Interior is advertising for bids for the construction of Division One, Garland Canal, Shoshone Irrigation Project, Wyoming. The work involves the excavation of about 600,000 cubic yards of earth, about 96,000 cubic yards of rock and shale, and the construction of the incidental structures, about 15 miles northeast of Cody, Wyoming.

DEPARTMENT OF THE INTERIOR.

Certificate of Filing
Water-Right Application.

Act June 17, 1902 (32 Stat., 388).

Amended Water Right, Graduated Payment, Notice Feby. 9, 1912.

Shoshone   PROJECT.

U. S. LAND OFFICE. Lander, Wyoming,   Serial No. 01811

March 13th, 1912

THIS IS TO CERTIFY That, pursuant to the provisions of the act of June 17, 1902 (32 Stat., 388),

Thomas Long, of Garland, Wyoming, has filed

application for Water Right (Form 4-031) for Farm Unit "W" Lot 5

(Whose land is in private ownership, strike out
the words "Farm Unit" and insert subdivisional description of land.)
                                                           , Section

Township 55 N., Range 98 W., 6th Principal   Meridian,

containing ----------59.91---------- acres of irrigable land,

In connection with Homestead Entry, Serial No. 01811, dated Nov. 5th, 1904,

(Strike out, when application is made on Form B, for land in private ownership.)

Now, therefore, be it known that, on presentation of this certificate to the Engineer of the U. S.

Reclamation Service in charge of the --------Shoshone--------Project, the

said applicant shall be entitled to receive, subject to the payment of the annual charges for building,

operation, and maintenance, --------3-------- acre feet of water per annum per acre of irrigable

land herein described, or so much thereof as shall constitute the proportionate share per acre from the

water supply actually available for the lands under said project: *Provided*, That the supply furnished

shall be limited to the amount of water beneficially used on said irrigable land.

William E. Adams

Register.

PAYMENTS.

No.	Date	Per cent of building	Date	Charge for operation and maintenance	Remarks
1					

Thomas Long's water right application with the Shoshone Irrigation Project, 1913.

Particulars may be obtained from the chief engineer of the Reclamation Service or from the engineer at Cody, Wyoming. The bids will be open May 24, at Billings, Mont. (NP1)

June 9, 1906 – One building at the Government Camp was completed this week, and the others will be completed as rapidly as possible. *The Guard* is informed that this camp will be maintained for at least three years. (NP1,NWN)

The Garland Division was finally opened for homesteading on November 25, 1907. 736 people began homesteading approximately 60,000 acres. (MA&P 2) On August 21, 1919, the Garland Division was reopened to add an additional 1,100 acres - 14 units to the north and east of Garland. (B10)

These early homesteaders were unsure, at first, of irrigation techniques, but they soon became masters of the process. Fay Smith recalls that her father had the art of irrigation down to a science.

"He had Mom make him canvas dams. He had her hem and make them so that he could put a rod through them so he could carry them that way. Other people nailed 2x4s and carried those big, old, heavy dams. My mom didn't like using her sewing machine for that, but I don't think it hurt it." (I25)

These little tricks helped the farmers grow their crops. By 1910, the Garland Division was growing alfalfa, potatoes, grain, sugar beets, beans, seed peas, apples, and other small fruits. (MA&P 2) In January of 1915, John Hendricks was elected president of the newly created Farmers Union. The farmers were producing enough produce that they needed to find markets for it. They also wanted to find

Henry Myers tending to Dido the cow and Jim and Bill, his trusted team of horses, in 1925.
Photo courtesy of Katie Brown.

a way to purchase seeds and other items that they couldn't grow themselves, at cheaper prices, by buying them in quantity. (B5)

As more and more of the land was being developed for farming, the cattle ranchers and sheepherders started to disappear. However, this does not mean that the livestock disappeared. The people of Garland were a self-sufficient group and needed their livestock, not only for food and extra income, but also to help with work around the farm. Many of the Garland residents interviewed remember stories, some fond and others not so fond, about the animals they had on the farm. Bonnie Hiller had to help with herding the cows and bringing them in at night. Fay Smith remembers milking the cow her family had.

"I always milked the cows twice a day. I don't know why the other girls didn't. Dad just picked me out. I didn't mind. It was good to get it done. I milked 3 or 4 cows both morning and night." (I25)

The residents of Garland learned, sometimes the hard way, that animals have minds of their own. Lloyd Killiam recalls a story about Mrs. Crane and her ornery Jersey bull.

"Mrs. Crane had a Jersey bull. Everybody worried about her because a Jersey bull can be very mean. He went on a rampage one day and pinned her to the fence. When she got up, she called a guy to come and get the bull. She was afraid. I remember when that guy backed the trailer up to the pen. He had one of those hotshots. He went into the pen, and Mrs. Crane warned him that the bull was mean. Armed with the hotshot, the guy yelled back, 'He won't be for long.' The bull started to charge. The guy touched him in the knee, [giving him] a strong shock from the hotshot. The bull turned, ran, and jumped the fence. So the guy jumped the fence and chased him back in. He made that bull jump the fence again and put him in the truck. The bull got rowdy in the truck, so the guy jabbed him again with the hotshot. Mrs. Crane hated to part with him; he was her baby. She had raised him from a little calf, but she knew she couldn't keep him." (I19)

Darwin Franklin tells the story of the day he was fishing with his brother, and Mr. Cross's mules were demonstrating just how stubborn mules (and their owners) can be.

"My brother and I were in the drain fishing; [there was] nice, cold, clear water and trout in it. (The drain ran right between Mr. Cross's farm and another one.) He was out loading hay by himself [that day] because he couldn't get anyone to help. He had a pair of mules hooked to the wagon, but the mules had a mind of their own. He would say, 'Ok boys, move up, move up.' We could hear him. He said, 'Move up. Come on fellas, be nice. Move up. Be good.' He had to go around and get a hold of them. 'Ok boys, move up.' … [They wouldn't budge an inch.] He got so angry with them but he didn't want to hit them, so he took a little bunch of hay and put it right under them. Then he put a match to it and set it on fire. They moved. They pulled the wagon up and over him. (He wasn't hurt.) We were already up out of the drain and ready to put out the fire. We were afraid it was going to catch his whole field on fire and run away." (I19)

Les Lawrence recalled a couple of stories about the animals he had around his place when he lived on the south side of the railroad tracks. He had five acres of land, but he didn't have any animals of his own. He let a family who lived in Garland pasture their three horses and pigs on his property. Les partnered with them and purchased 200 baby chicks. This arrangement kept things interesting on the farm for a while.

"I had [put] in a garden, and one day the pigs and their little pigs got out. The little pigs were just big enough to run around real good. They found that garden, and they just went right down every row. They destroyed it. So we got rid of the little pigs in a hurry." (I21)

"That same family had three boys. The middle boy was very ambitious and thought they should have some turkeys. He had heard about white turkeys and was really interested in them. He went to the experimental station at the college (NWC). They got some eggs, put them in an incubator, and hatched about 15 white turkeys. So he wanted to bring them out. I said, 'There is no way to control them. You don't want to put them in a building.' But he figured that out. He built a pen, with woven wire and put a top on it. It was light enough that you could move it, with about three or four people to help. He brought those turkeys out and moved them every day or so to different, green patches of grass. One day a big wind came up, and it soon was snowing - a blizzard. We were all in town. When we got home, the cage had blown over, and the turkeys were gone. So we called the boy, and his family came out to look for them. We didn't find all of them. I think we could only find five. The next morning, we got up, and the rest were all paired up. They were next to the fence, and we got all of them." (I21)

Sometimes the livestock were used as a way to supplement the family's income. The sale of meat or eggs gave the family a little extra money to purchase the extras that weren't necessarily needed, or to help with the bills. Bonnie Hiller's mother raised turkeys so that she could buy a little something for the house and help pay for the groceries.

"My mother raised turkeys. She would have quite a flock of them. She raised them with the idea of buying something for the house. I can remember that she bought what we called a library table with her turkey money. I can't remember what else, but most of the time, it [her earnings] went to pay the grocery bill. (In the summer they would run a grocery bill at the Garland store.) I know my mother vowed, after we were all gone from home, [that] she was never going to have another grocery bill. They were going to pay as they went. The farmers, so many times, waited on the crops to come in. That was the way you lived. (I15)

There were several crops that were raised and are still being raised in the Garland area today: alfalfa, grain, sugar beets, potatoes, beans, sunflowers, and even some fruit (mostly apples). Fruit has never been a cash crop, but if people are lucky enough to keep their trees alive through the first frost, the fruit is a welcome treat. J.S. Brown not only got his fruit trees through the first frost, but his orchard was even successful enough to start selling fruit trees.

Stacking hay. August 1912. Photo courtesy Shoshone Irrigation District Photo Archives.

Loading hay with buck rakes. August, 1912. Photo courtesy Shoshone Irrigation District Photo Archives.

October 28, 1905 - Fruit Trees for Sale - The Undersigned has for sale a choice lot of yearling apple trees of a very hardy variety, especially acclimated for the Big Horn Basin climate. Will sell for cash or exchange for grain, allowing the market price for the grain. Price per tree, 10 cents. Write me at Ionia, Big Horn Co., Wyo. J.S. Brown. Ionia. (NP1)

By 1918 – 1919, the favored apple producers were Bishop William Partridge of Cowley and Frank Hart from Garland. People of the Basin were making wagon trips to Cowley and Garland for their apples. The apples were then canned or dried for the winter. (B10)

Alfalfa was one of the first cash crops in the area. The soil in the Garland Division had poor nutrients, but alfalfa could still be grown there, giving the families a source of income while also building up the soil for other crops to be grown later on. Still, by February of 1915, due to the allure of much faster growing Powell, Garland had started to see a decline, but once again alfalfa came to the rescue. There were plans to build two alfalfa mills, one in each of the neighboring communities. This meant that farmers would have a place to dispose of their alfalfa, and it also gave them a new employer as well. Many farmers worked in the mill, during the winter months, to earn a little extra income for their families. It brought a lot of hope to the community, as reported in *The Powell Tribune.*

February, 1915 - Garland may be a dead one, but it certainly has great hopes of soon coming back to life. Two alfalfa mills are coming, and these alone will help make things boom. The farmers around town are all glad to have these mills come, as it will afford them some place to dispose of their alfalfa. (NP2)

April 23, 1915 – Good news for everybody this week. Mr. Ames, the alfalfa mill man is here and he tells us they will begin building the mill right away. We certainly hope it won't be long until the mill is at work. (NP2)

June 25, 1915 – Our alfalfa mill is well underway. The well was completed last week, and this week, they are making the foundation. (NP2)

By September of 1915, the mills in Powell and Garland were both operational. Farmers were paid $6.50 per ton for hay delivered to the mill and were able to get three cuttings per season. They stacked the alfalfa in the fields and allowed it to cure during the summer months. Cecilia Hennel Hendricks explains how the hay was harvested in her book, *Letters from Honeyhill: A Woman's View of Homesteading:*

Aug 1, 1916 – Hay is stacked in the field or barn lot. The people who raise hay regularly use a stacker. This is simply a large, wooden-toothed affair that lifts the hay up in the air by means of a beam and rope, the rope pulled by a horse. The stacker drops the hay on the stack. The horse is then backed till the stacking fork lies on the ground again. But for folks without a stacker, the "Mormon method" is used. When the hay is loaded on the wagons in the field, a rope is laid across the rack so that a loop hangs down the center side, and the two ends hang down on the other side. When the wagon comes to the haystack, the ends of the rope are slipped through the loop and the hay on the load, is thus bound together. Another large rope is fastened to this rope, the large rope leading over the stack and out on the other side, where a team of horses is hitched to it. The horses are driven on, and the whole load from the wagon is rolled up on the stack, at once. It can be rolled as far over on the stack as desired, merely by driving the horses farther. That saves practically all the usual pitching from the wagon to the stack. It is interesting to see a great load roll over and up on top of the stack. The stack in our barn lot, that the men put up yesterday and today, is 40x16x20 feet high. (B5)

When winter approached, farmers hauled the alfalfa from the fields to the mill, baled or loose. (B5) Lloyd Killiam remembers the fun they had as kids with the hay wagons, running back and forth to the mill.

The alfalfa mill provided an extra job for many farmers in the area. Newspaper clipping courtesy of Irma Yonts.

"We would take our sleds. We had a rope that was long enough so we could hold on to one end of it. They always had a loop on the back of the wagon. We would stick the rope through that loop and sit there and hang on. We would ride into the country 2 or 3 miles and catch the next wagon coming back to town. On Saturdays, we would do that all day long. If you wanted to stop, you just turned the rope loose. The farmer knew we were there. He would [even] make the horses trot once in awhile." (I19)

At the mill, the hay was pitched from the wagons onto the conveyor belt that was approximately 100 to 150 feet long. The hay was ground into alfalfa meal, and then was bagged and loaded onto the railcars, to be shipped to market. All of the equipment was run by coal-fired steam engines. (I13) If the supply of hay were too much for the mill to process, a covered hay rack was available to store the excess until it could be ground. This also ensured locals of employment during the winter months. (I22)

In January of 1916, the mill was still grinding, and the farmers were almost finished delivering their hay. The mill was expected to run through the end of the month and was shipping out about five cars per day. By mid-February, all of the hay was ground, and the mill was closed for the season. (NP2) In June of 1916, after some minor repairs, the mill was reopened for business.

June 16, 1916 – The Omaha Alfalfa Milling Co., is installing a steam loader at their mill here, in the near future. (NP2)

June 30, 1916 – The hay harvest has begun in earnest. Everyone is haying now. The crop is excellent, for the cold spring and summer we have had. A new coat of paint has been added to the alfalfa mill, which improves its looks a great deal. (NP2)

Hay at the Powell alfalfa mill. Photo courtesy Shoshone Irrigation District Photo Archives.

Hay at the Powell alfalfa mill. September, 1914. Photo courtesy Shoshone Irrigation District Photo Archives.

The 1916 – 1917 winter season was tough on the mill. In August, crews started hauling hay from Otto Smith's fields west of Garland, but, by September, the mill was closed for ten days, due to a lack of manpower. In November, it was up and running again, but by January of 1917, the workers were cleaning the hay out of the sheds. In March, *The Powell Tribune* reported that two area farmers were shipping their hay to Powell instead of using the Garland Mill. From the articles in *The Powell Tribune*, it seems that after 1917, the Garland enterprise was an on again, off again industry which apparently had shut down in 1919, as after that, no further mention is ever made of it.

In Garland's early years, potatoes were another important crop. *The Garland Guard* ran an article in May of 1906 advertising that "fine potatoes can be had in any quantity, at Bowler, Mont., for $1.25." "A good chance to get your seed potatoes and start farming." (NP1) Over ten years later, *The Powell Tribune* was reporting that potato growers were busy harvesting, selling, and shipping out several car loads of potatoes every day. (NP2)

November 7, 1917 – Some potato growers have cellars or caves made with concrete walls and earth roofs to keep their potatoes until spring. The main bulk of the potatoes are sold right from the field. They are piled and covered with straw and earth until they are hauled to the cars. (NP2)

As young boys growing up in Garland Jim Hart and his brother Hubert helped their father raise potatoes. Jim remembered potato harvest as time-consuming, hard work. He recalled school being released for a couple of weeks so that the children could help with the harvest. Jim talked about the family's first potato digger, which was pulled by two, or maybe three horses and only dug one row at a time. The blade was the size of the potato row, and it dug into the ground under the potatoes. It pulled them out of the ground, onto the conveyor, and then dropped them back on the ground again.

Sometimes the blade didn't get into the ground low enough or would get off the row. This caused the blade to cut the potatoes. If this happened, they couldn't be shipped. These potatoes were thrown out or used by the family. In later years, Jim's family purchased a two-row digger that was pulled behind a tractor.

Raising mostly Bliss Triumph potatoes, Jim continued the family tradition of potato farming. He refurbished the alfalfa mill, turning it into a potato plant. The potatoes were stored and washed in the plant, and shipped on railroad cars to Jim's broker, The Michael Bronson Brady Company, in Kansas City, Missouri. The potato plant had a Thompson potato grader/shaker. The potatoes bumped along the conveyor in shakers or baskets and were thrown over to the screen. Angular openings in the screen allowed dirt and small potatoes to fall out. The small potatoes were put aside as seed potatoes for the next year. The sunburned or cut potatoes were picked out by hand. The remaining potatoes continued down the conveyor and filled potato sacks. When each sack was full, a board in the middle of the grader would turn, moving the next sack into place. While one sack was filling, someone would put the empty sack in line. Each sack was weighed to make sure that it was close to 100 pounds. Then it was loaded onto wagons or trucks and hauled to the awaiting railcar. Jim ran his business for several years. During World War II, he had people from the Heart Mountain Relocation Camp come to help with the harvest. In about 1950, a rumor was circulated that there was something wrong with the Hart potatoes. Jim never was sure what the rumor was, but his business never recovered and was forced to close the potato plant. (I13)

Beets were and still are a major crop in the Garland area. Beet harvest, while still challenging at times, is considerably easier now than it was when everything was done by hand. After wagons or trucks were filled with beets, they were sent to the Garland beet dump. It was a large dump and people from all over shipped their beets from there. Garland residents regarded that beet dump with some apprehension. Merl Fales remembers the early years of the dump:

A crew digging potatoes on D. Harrison's farm unit in the Garland Division. September 10, 1925. Photo courtesy Shoshone Irrigation District Photo Archives.

"The beet dump was north of the railroad tracks. As you are leaving Garland, it was on the right side of the road, close to the tracks. I would come down there in the morning, about the time we were supposed to be getting on the school bus. The beet dump was open, and they would have a fire built because it was fall and chilly. The teams would pull in with loads of beets. They had to put on an extra team of horses to pull the load up and down the beat dump ramp. It was kind of spooky up there. It was a pine-built structure, and it rattled and rattled until you got to the top. It felt like you were kind of in outer space up there. There was a guy on the ground, driving one team, and another guy driving the team on top. When you got up to the top, you dumped your load into a box car, an open-topped railroad car. Then they used the extra team of horses and a lot of brake to get the wagon back down. It was steep." (I7)

Burchell Hopkin has fond memories of the beet dump. He often rode in the truck with his father to Garland. His father would give him a penny and Burchell would go to the store to buy something.

"It was a great, tall thing with a long incline that the truck drove up. You got high enough that you dumped into the railroad car. The only dirt you got back was what fell through the grate as they [the beets] spilled into the car."

While beet harvest is a little easier today and the dump sites are not quite so intimidating, it is still easy to identify with those who used them years ago. Lucy Cozzens recalls a muddy September harvest and why she enjoyed driving truck so much:

"I hauled beets for Mr. Cubbage for several years. One year, we had a big snow in September. (I think we got more ice than anything.) They had the dump in Garland [then]. People came from north and south of Garland. It [the dump] was right there by the railcars. There were big balls of mud everywhere. It was muddy work, but it gave me a little extra income and some entertainment, as I stood around talking to people waiting in line to dump. (I4)

Beans were also an important crop and helped the author's great grandmother pay off her farm after the loss of her husband. *The Powell Tribune* reported in 1936 that Bessie Gimmeson and her six children had the pleasure of burning the mortgage for their 40-acre farm in the Shoshone Irrigation District. Their farm was purchased for $3,100 in 1928. According to Ernest J. Goppert, Secretary Treasurer of the Cody National Farm Loan association, Mrs. Gimmeson's management of the farm and the proceeds from a good bean crop helped to pay off the $1000 remaining on the mortgage, after Mr. Gimmeson's death. Goppert is quoted as saying, "Mrs. Gimmeson has done a good job of managing, and she is entitled to a lot of credit."

The way crops were harvested altered dramatically with the change from horses to tractors. Early on, most homestead parcels consisted of only about 40 acres because that was about all that could be plowed with horses. (I6) When tractors came into use, more land could be put into production. Not only did it affect the farm production, but also the way wives planned for meals. Bonnie Hiller explains how preparation for meals changed with the coming of the tractor:

Truck load of sugar beets in a field in the Garland Division. September, 1930. Photo courtesy Shoshone Irrigation District Photo Archives.

"Mom and I laughed about the way women's chores and mealtime changed from the days when my dad farmed with horses to when he got his first tractor. Let's say the crew stopped for lunch. You still had some time. First, they unhooked the horses. Then they had to water and feed them. Mom said that with the tractor, they just shut the thing off, and there they were. She taught me long ago always to set the table, and I have never forgotten that. If a man comes in and sees the table set, he figures food is not far behind, whether you're ready or not. If the table is set, that buys you a little bit of time. At least, they think food is on the way.

"And, of course, in those days, crews went from farm to farm and you cooked a big dinner for them. They had what they called their "run" and certain farms banded together. You didn't hire anybody. Everybody banded together to help each other with the harvest. Mother would say she thought the men liked to tell you what they ate at the last person's place, so you would try to outdo that woman with the feed you put out. (My mother was noted for her cooking.) (I15)

The Starr beet dump bridge. 1930. Photo courtesy The Homesteader Museum.

The Meyers family showing off their corn crop. Photo courtesy of Katie Brown.

There were several styles of the early tractors. Warren Cubbage talked a little about the Staude Mak-a-tractor. He remembered that you put metal wheels on your Ford, giving it good traction and then you could pull farm implements with it. In Cecilia Hennel Hendricks's book, *Letters from Honeyhill*, she describes the Staude Mak-a-tractor in detail.

We got two gears for it, one for road-hauling and one for tractor work, in plowing. The road gear makes the machines run much faster than the plowing gear. The road speed is five miles an hour. I think the plow speed is less than half that. But even at that, the machine is supposed to plow from five to seven acres a day, in a ten-hour day. That beats a team or a couple teams, all to pieces. The tractor part is easily attached to the Ford. There are three parts that stay on the Ford permanently: one is a force-feed oiling system that makes the oiling on the auto like that of high priced autos. Another is a frame of heavy iron that fits on the under part of the chassis of the Ford, and on which that tractor rear axle works. The third is a radiator that is eleven times as powerful as the usual Ford radiator. (The more you reduce the speed the better the radiator has to be to keep the engine properly cooled.) These three parts stay on the auto; there are two hubs with bearings in them, one for each back wheel. Then, there are two large eight-inch tire iron wheels connected by a strong axle, that fits in, to work on these bearings. When you have the first three mentioned parts permanently attached, all you do to turn your Ford into a tractor, is to take off the

The Meyers children out on the farm. From left to right: Katie, Loretta, Clara, Ethel and Bud, in the car.
Photo courtesy of Katie Brown.

hind wheels, fit in the bearing hubs, and bolt the two, big tractor wheels with their axles on. It is quite simple. (B5)

Jim Hart remembered that several farmers in the community had Fordson tractors. He remembered them as being small, but not very versatile. They had two big drive wheels, low gears, and a maximum speed of ten miles per hour. They were best used for plowing. Jim also remembered a number of makeshift farm tractors like the Staude Mak-a-tractor. (I13) Jack VanLake believed that his father had the first gasoline run tractor in the Garland area. He has a picture of his father on it when Standard Oil brought gas to him. It had spiked wheels. (I26) Fay Smith remembered her father's big Case tractor and the day she she tore up the hay mower. She accidentally ran the mower into an end post. Luckily, her father was a good mechanic and didn't get too angery. (I25)

Fay was just one of many children who helped around the farm. The children were an enormous help and a necessity. They worked as laborers, assisting with weeding and the harvest. Ethel Heimer remembers her father trying to arrange harvesting on the weekends, so the children wouldn't miss school. However, Merl Fales remembers missing school, in the fall, to help run a team of horses, during threshing.

"When I was 12 years old, I could take a team of horses and run a wagon when we threshed our place. The rest were all men running the threshing equipment. I could go out there, and I knew how to stack those beans on that wagon, so they wouldn't fall off and shatter, better than some of them, because I'm a thresher. I filled that wagon up. Then I would drive to that spooky machine, the feeder. The horses didn't want to go up there too much. I would drive them up there, chalk them up, do up my line, get my pitchfork, and look over at the next wagon across on the other side. The driver of the other wagon might have been there for awhile, but I wanted to leave him there [and finish first]. My boss said he didn't know anybody that wanted to work like that, but it paid off." (I17)

Fay Smith and Bonnie Hiller both regard with dread the horrible chore of weeding. Bonnie remembers spending days pulling cockleburs, crawling on her hands and knees through the fields, with knee pads that her mother made. To this day, she still pulls them up if she sees them. Fay fondly recalls how wonderful a swim in the cold canal felt at night, after a hot day of weeding.

Farming and ranching were hard work, but they brought the community of Garland together. Working side-by-side, residents got their harvests in and offered a helping hand whenever one was needed. Even today, the people of Garland are willing to pitch in when necessary or let a neighbor borrow a piece of equipment. Each new generation deals with some of the same challenges as those who came before them, and just as they did, works together, with the same community spirit that has always made the area bloom.

Chapter 6 - Weather: It Happens

Wyoming has four very diverse seasons, but marked daily weather variations are commonplace and often unexpected. Since most of the state is rural and agronomic or mineral dependent, this can present challenges, which, in the early years, were especially daunting. Weather extremes and flooding and drought promoted an innovative spirit, strength of character, and a "can do" attitude in Wyoming's people. Small town residents, in particular, learned to depend on one another, during rain, hail, sleet, or snow.

In talking with Garland residents, one thing becomes increasingly clear: winters used to be much more severe than they are today. Snow fell deep enough to cover fence posts, the air was colder, and people had to shovel pathways to their outbuildings. The following winters seem to stick out in the minds of the local residents: 1886, 1906, 1917, 1919, 1948, and 1978. The winter of 1886/87 was the worst ever recorded on the Northern Plains. Several ranchers lost part or all of their livestock. This is the winter that changed open range grazing forever. (B11) Twenty years later, signs in nature predicted another bad winter. *The Garland Guard* reported these observations.

October 7, 1905 – The Indians on the Crow Reservation are predicting a hard winter this season. (NP1)

October 14, 1905 – All signs point to a hard winter, and from indications last Sunday, it will not only be a hard, but also a long one. Now is the time to prepare for it. (NP1)

October 21, 1905 – Coyotes are becoming very numerous with the advent of cold weather. (NP1)

In the spring, residents stopped to reflect on the winter. It had been a bad one, as expected, but it had been worse for people who lived outside of the sheltered Bighorn Basin.

March 17, 1906 – The Basin Freighters have been hung up here for several days, waiting for the cessation of the hostilities, on the part of old Borealis. The passenger train from the north was ten hours late on Wednesday, by reason of the blizzard raging that day. When we read of accounts of the great March storm throughout the country, we feel led to shake hands with ourselves and congratulate ourselves that we live in the Bighorn Basin of Wyoming, for while we apparently got all that was coming to us, other sections suffered much more than we, and for us, the Bighorn sun still shines. (NP1)

The winter of 1917 made headlines in *The Powell Tribune*. On February 2, *The Tribune* reported that the winter had been the worst any of the inhabitants had seen yet. On the other hand, in such a dry climate, it is not a surprise that, in the same article, the heavy snowfall had been praised as being good for the fields, (especially the alfalfa), and the orchards, and the rangeland that the cattle and sheep would graze on in the spring and summer. (NP2)

Robert White chronicles in his book, *The Frannie-Deaver Proposition,* that the winter of 1919 was an especially hard one. It started to snow on October 18, and bad weather continued into December. when temperatures reached 32 degrees below zero. The storm was accompanied by a fuel shortage. The Pine Bluff Coal Mine worked at capacity but could not get enough coal out of the ground to keep up with the demand. Rationing was put in place. The Powell merchants shortened their hours, and the pool hall closed early. Families were only allowed a 100-pound gunny-sack full of coal instead of a wagonload apiece. The blizzard and heavy snow also crippled the mail coming into the Basin. (B10)

When asked for his recollections, Les Lawrence replied that the winter of 1955 was the worse winter in his memory. He particularly remembered one storm and the difficulty of getting from Powell to his farm in Garland to take care of his livestock.

"That one big storm got to 45 degrees below! I stayed with my wife's family in Powell but had to come out and feed the horses. It was all I could do to get out there. The snow was getting deeper all the time. It drifted in some places, some places were three feet. Another day, it was about 40 degrees below. The rest of the time, it was about 30 below. That was the worst weather I have ever seen. That was around 1955 or somewhere in there." (I21)

Warren and Johanna Cubbage say the winter of 1978 was one of the last bad winters. They remember there being a lot of snow and that it just kept piling up. Warren commented on the fact that there was so much snow that the plows could hardly keep the roads plowed. (I6)

No matter how cold or how snowy, the residents of Garland coped with it and sometimes even found ways to have fun with it. Several residents remember shoveling trails to the chicken coop, the root cellar, and the outhouse. Ethel Heimer says it took a long time for things to thaw in the spring, with temperatures still below zero. She also remembers her father keeping the path to the root cellar clear so that they could get to their provisions. (I14). Darwin Franklin says that when there was too much snow on the roads, the residents made their own.

"We used to have snow, and snow would pile up along the county road. It looked big to us kids. These roads were snowed in lots of times before there was a highway out here. To get around the snow, people came through the field on our place, to find an easy way to cross it. This became the new road until the snow melted."

Herb Jones and Hubert Hart also recall that snow got so deep that it drifted onto their roads. Hubert tells of drifts as high as the school bus in 1929. He also remembers the roads being rerouted through their fields. (I12) Herb says that people sometimes left their cars in the highway because drifts along the country roads were deep enough to cover fenceposts, making it impossible to get a car up or down them. He remembers barely getting out even with horses, because they would bog down in the snow. Walking out wasn't any easier either, so people would wait it out during these times, as there weren't many snowplows to clear the way. (I8)

Still the winter weather was not all bad. Many residents retain cherished memories from the winters of their youth. They remember games played in the schoolyard and snowflakes made from catalogue pages. Moms would make ice cream treats by adding vanilla and sugar to the snow. There were sleigh rides to the school when the snow was too deep for the bus, and also sledding on the creek in the snow. Ice skating was a memory shared by most residents too. Some skated in the gravel pit, while others preferred the area down by the Brown's. The Brown family knew how to make winter fun for everyone. They took advantage of the cold weather and made a community ice skating rink east of their home:

"Good old Wyoming weather. You just never know. But growing up, we used to enjoy the creek. We used to sled some there. And then someone got Dad to flood an area over in the old pasture. I believe there was a drain that came in there - maybe, one of those closed drains that came in there. They could flood the area, and we had a skating rink down there. And the kids from the community and some of them from Powell used to gather down there - Will Scott, the Stanley boys, the Hiemers, and the Meyer girls. Everybody would come over there, and we would build fires down along there. Some would have hot chocolate and things, but we would skate on that pond in the wintertime." (I15)

Lloyd Killiam remembers the skating pond and the fun he had there:

"And then we would have skating parties. When it got cold, we would go over by the Brown place, down on the creek. They had a community ice skating rink. The skating rink was in kind of a damp place. Sometimes we would get off the bus on Thursday night and give it a fresh shot of water, so it would be good for the weekend. That was big entertainment, our skating." (I19)

While fun, the residents knew that winter was also dangerous. Bonnie Hiller has a great respect for winter. She tells stories of two frigid winter experiences - one from her childhood and one that occurred when she was an adult with children. The first she tells is about her youngest brother. She tells of when he fell through the ice, while sledding on the creek. She remembers him going under water and being hit in the chest by a chunk of ice. When he was pulled to safety and brought to the house, he was very cold and could hardly breathe. The family was worried about him, but after he warmed up, he was alright. The second story happened after she was married and had four children of her own. (This story might motivate readers to carry warm clothing in their cars - rain, snow, or shine.)

"One Easter Sunday, Loren, the girls, and I had gone to church and stayed in town at Harry and Janet Wilkins, and, of course, we were all in our Easter finery, with no fall boots or anything. We were only five miles away from home. We started down our road, and the car stalled. The snow-drifts were too deep, so Loren carried Kathy and Sandra and walked to the house. I stayed in the car with Sheri, who was a baby at that time, and Marilyn. When he came back, Loren would carry Marilyn, and I would carry the baby. It seemed like they had been walking for a long time. Then I finally saw that yardlight go on at home. When Loren came back to the car, he said there was no way I could walk, much less carry the baby. He said he had fallen several times with Kathy. But he had called Jerry Wilson, who worked for the city, and he and Bud Steele came out with a truck, weighed down with rocks, and dragged us home." (I15)

Summer, while not as dangerous, isn't any easier to make predictions about. The weather during this season can have a huge effect on the local economy. Late frosts, hail, flooding, and even lightning, can ruin a whole year's worth of crops. Jack VanLake's father told him about the year Garland got a late frost on June 30th. It ruined the bean crop for that year. (I26) Hail often wiped out crops too and could also be hard on the livestock. Herb Jones tells of the hail storm on August 14, 1952. The beans and hay were just about ready to be cut when the hail went right through the flat. After it was all over, all Herb had left was two sacks of beans and some hay. Thankfully he was able to salvage the ruined beans and use them for seed beans for the next three years. That year, he had to find a winter job. He was not alone. Everyone north of the Shoshone River was wiped out. The storm ruined oats, grain, and beets, as well. (I18) Merl and Colette Gimmeson remembered that storm. It came too late to replant anything. Colette can still remember the smell of the rotting radish field across the road from the house. (I11)

In a dry environment like the Garland area, it is hard to believe flooding would be a problem, but it has been, since its beginnings. *The Garland Guard* reports the dangers and problems that flooding caused in 1906.

June 16, 1906 – *Rivers are Flooded. Shoshone and Greybull go on a Rampage. Garland Bridge - Safe and Sound.* Reports from all over the Basin tell of an unprecedented rise in the waters of the Shoshone and Greybull Rivers. At Worland, a young man by the name of Smort, who was tending the ferry, was drowned, and travelers from that way report that the water was spreading over the banks rapidly at Otto; the bridge is in perilous condition.

At Corbett, the old bridge, which has been in use for a long time, finally went out on Wednesday. At Cody, the bridge was saved only by hard work, for a period of 48 hours by piling sacks of sand and rock upon it.

At Garland, the report was brought in that rock had washed out the center bridge pier and [that] Thos. Long, through the initiative of calling for volunteers to go down and refill, thus put it out of danger. Two teams were speedily offered, and Thursday afternoon, they were manned by a force of Garland men who proceeded to the river. When they arrived, they found that Mr. Hopkin already had a small force of men and teams at work. With the assistance of the Garland force, the work was soon completed. Those from Garland were Carl Long, Ralph Naylor, D. McCulloch, J.F. Jensen, A. Jones, H. Holman, H. Hopkins with team, Paxton Lowe with a team, Dwight King, Vern King, Russell Denny, Carl Wilson, J. Stafford, J. Fay, Dr. Cole, John Hopkins, and G.A. Phip.

Later … The bridge at Otto went out at 9:00 am Thursday. A 6-horse freight outfit was on it when it went down. The men and horses escaped, but the load will probably be a total loss. The wagons are lodged on a sand bar. The same day, the new railroad bridge at Lovell was washed down the stream several feet, delaying the completion of the road to Worland. (NP1)

Over the years, the bridges around Garland have often been sacrificed to rising flood water. Bonnie Hiller remembers that heavy rain took the bridge near their house more than once. Flooding also took out the bridge at Garland numerous times. Bonnie can recall watching water lapping against and over the highway bridge that crosses Bitter Creek, west of Garland.

Some of our summer rainstorms are accompanied by lightning. In the evenings, a good summer lightning storm is a beautiful thing to watch, but it can also be intimidating. Bonnie Hiller remembers that kind of lightning storms from her youth.

"We used to have some pretty good electric storms. I remember one time dad thought we were on fire. He could smell smoke. Lightning had hit a post to the north of us, in the field, and set the post on fire.

On another occasion, when I lived at the old house, we had an electric storm, and I was at the old cook stove. All at once, my lights went out, and I heard the crash of glass. I thought my light bulb had blown out, but it was the fuse box in the kitchen. The electricity had come in and blown that fuse box out - blackening it.

Us kids were always scared of electricity and wondered if it would strike an animal. Our big collie dog - he was afraid of it too. e would try to get just as close to you as he could get." (I15)

The opposite of flooding - drought - seems to be such a regular occurrence that many residents didn't have much to say about it. They all agreed that the irrigation system here has been a lifesaver and one way of easing the unpredictability of the weather.

The people of Garland have learned to cope with the weather and enjoy it most of the time. Just about everyone appreciates a good snowstorm, with plenty of snow for sledding, a wonderful summer evening lightning storm, or an occasional showing of the Northern Lights. Many arrive unannounced.

Colette Gimmeson has the most logical approach about the weather and the impact it has had and continues to have on our lives. She said: "There were some good years and some bad years. It will always be that way, I guess."

And, of course she is absolutely right.

Chapter 7 - Keeping Warm

"Everybody kept warm out of that hole in the ground." - Ted Lord

During the long Wyoming winters, one resource was of great importance - coal. John Hopkin located a coal mine four miles north of Garland, shortly after the town was established. He was the first of many who would attempt to keep Garland and the surrounding communities warm by hauling coal out of what is today referred to as Coal Mine Hill. The business of coal mining was not a steady proposition. It was hard work with many difficulties to overcome. Still, coal was mined and hauled off that hill until the late 1950's, when the government came and filled in the mine shafts, for fear of cave-ins.

John Hopkin knew what he was looking for, as he had done some coal mining and locating in Utah before coming to Garland. His scouting in the Basin led to the discovery of a vein just west of Coal Mine Hill, below Polecat Bench. He started mining and selling on a small scale, and eventually added a coal car to his operation. Coal was pulled out of the mine by a horse that was hitched to a sweep, which wound a rope around a drum.

The coal from this mine was not the best quality. It produced too much ash, but it made good heat. Burchell Hopkin doesn't think that his grandfather, John, ever made a big fortune from his efforts. He has looked for mining claims from the time when his grandfather first started mining but has been unable to find anything. He is not sure if John sold his interest in the mine or just walked away from it. (I16)

The area John Hopkin had mined became known as The Pine Bluff Coal Company, named after the scrub pines that used to surround it. (I17) The next owner was Joseph Neville who leased it to John Pryde. Pryde then worked the mine successfully for several years.

November 18, 1905 – The writer took a trip out to the coal mine of the Pine Bluff Coal Company on Tuesday in the company of Com. Neville, who is one of the principal owners of the mine. We looked the proposition over thoroughly, and what we saw was a revelation to our vision. The mine is now nearly 200 feet in, on the mountain, and the entrance to the mine is almost level, thus making the taking out of coal a very easy matter. The worker, Mr. Pryde, who has two-year lease on the property, is now shifting to the right, at about two thirds [of the way] in from the entrance, where he is working on a 3 1/2 foot ledge of as fine a coal as is being mined anywhere in the Basin. The ledge is absolutely free from rock, and the coal is of a very hard variety which will harden as greater depth is reached. The company has a splendid chute and dump, and wagons can be loaded with very little work. The writer brought some of the coal down from the mine and made a thorough test of it, and we unhesitatingly pronounce it as good as any coal we have ever used. The mine is very easy to access and is especially favorably located for Cowley and Lovell people, as it is a good road and downgrade all the way. Three or four tons can be hauled down with one outfit. (NP1)

By December, the coal from the Pine Bluffs Mine was readily available for purchase. The price was $2.50 per ton at the mine. Coal could be delivered at a higher rate. Orders were to be left at Joseph Neville's office in Garland. (NP1)

As the Pine Bluffs Mine was getting started, Joseph Neville had his sights on another mine and was trying to get stockholders to buy into it, as well. The new company was to be called the Gate City Coal Company. Many of the Pine Bluff investors were involved in the newly organized company. In October of 1905, the Gate City Coal Company was organizing for permanent business in the city of Garland. The principal stock had been purchased by prosperous Germania parties. Mr. Wunderlich was the largest stockholder. Along with their purchase, Germania backers were also to be the work force behind the mine. They were planning to use a traction engine to hoist the coal out of the ground. As the weather was turning colder, the demand for coal was increasing. The Gate City Coal Company had backing and a work force. The only thing left to be done was an inspection of the site, so they turned to Mr. Pryde, who, was the local expert.

October 28, 1905 – Commissioner Neville and Mr. Pryde, an expert on coal mine development, on Wednesday went up to the Neville-Lampman coal claim to inspect the property with a view to opening up and developing the claim immediately. Mr. Pryde, after a thorough inspection of the grounds, pronounced it one of the best prospects in the state, as a result of which developing the claim will be prosecuted with vigor, beginning next week. This sounds like business. (NP1)

That was not soon enough for the residents of Garland. Winter was setting in, and there wasn't sufficient coal to go around. Some of the residents would have to get it from other sources. There were three articles with regard to the coal situation in the November 4 issue of *The Garland Guard.*

November 4, 1905 – A car load of coal has at last arrived, and, as a result, the backbone of the coal famine, is broken. By the time this car is gone, local coal will be upon the market. (NP1)

November 4, 1905 – *The Guard* man yesterday called upon Treasurer, Dave McCulloch, of the Gate City Coal Company, and made inquires as to when work on the company's claims near Garland would begin. We were informed that work would commence immediately upon the reorganization of the board of directors, which will take place at the meeting of the board, which has been called for next Saturday afternoon. (NP1)

November 4, 1905 – Commissioner Neville, James Howell, and the Messrs. Lampman have begun active development work on their coal property west of town and before long, there will be plenty of coal on the local market. Mr. John Pryde, of Byron, has taken a lease upon the property and will hasten development work with all possible speed. Mr. Pryde is one of the best coal miners and experts in the West, and he would not have attempted such a task unless it was a genuine proposition. In fact, he pronounces the claim as one of the best he has seen, judging from indications on the surface and having given similar properties a thorough study. He is in a position to know what this claim means to promoters. (NP1)

Coal mine near Garland. August, 1929. Photos courtesy of the Shoshone Irrigation District photo archives.

People continued to work to get both the Pine Bluffs and the Gate City Mines open. During the stockholders' meeting on November 11, the Gate City Mine Company was reorganized. A.C. Wunderlich, of Germania, became the president and resident agent; H.A. Wegner, of Germania, the secretary; D. A. McCulloch, the treasurer; and George Shoemaker, the business manager. During the meeting, it was decided that the company would spend nearly $2000 toward improvements, including a hoisting engine, which would also be used to pump the water out of the mine. (This was a problem that would haunt all the mines on Coal Mine Hill, until they were closed.) A force of men would be employed, working steadily in two shifts. Dave McCoulloch, Mike Healey, and Mr. Conrat were just a few of the men employed by the mine. John Thorpe was given the contract to haul lumber to the mine for bracing. He traveled to the Pryor Mountains to cut timbers for stabilization of the shaft. Finally, after reorganization and a lot of hard work, *The Garland Guard* reported on November 11, that there would soon be plenty of coal available from both the Gate City and Pine Bluff Coal Companies.

November 11, 1905 – The new coal mine, now being developed by Messrs Neville, Howell ,and Lampman, which is being worked by Mr. John Pryde, lessee, expects to have coal on the market, at the mine, by next Monday, announcement of which will be made later on. The coal is said to be of an exceptionally fine quality. (NP1)

By December of 1905, however, a third coal mine appeared to have sneaked into the mix. A December article was the first mention of it in *The Guard*. This could be due to the fact that faith in the surrounding coal companies seemed to be faltering. The mines appear to have been unable to surmount the hurdles that kept production from materializing. This had to have been devastating to everyone.

December 2, 1905 – There are three mines within three to six miles of Garland, and all are supposed to be working, yet nary a pound of coal can you get, for love or money. Some would make money with a coal agency here and have coal shipped in from Sheridan. (NP1)

On December 9, *The Garland Guard* again reported that there was still no coal to be found. By December 16, *The Guard* was praising E.C. Spencer for making arrangements to have several rail cars of Monarch lump coal brought in. Citizens were able to purchase this coal by the ton or by car lots. Spencer worked with them on the price. (NP1)

Although *The Garland Guard* seems to lose interest and does not follow their progress after the December 16 article, the mines continued to struggle through the rest of the winter. In March of 1906, there is some evidence that they may have been shut down for a time.

March 10, 1906 – At a meeting of the Gate City Coal Company held on Monday, it was agreed to again operate the mine. Work will be resumed at once. (NP1)

Throughout their history, the mines at Coal Mine Hill continued to rise and fall. *The Powell Tribune* reported that the Farmers' Union was having coal shipped in on the train during the winter of 1916-1917. It does not mention whether the mines were shut down or just unable to keep up with the demand.

January 21, 1916 – The Farmers' Union received a car of coal on Saturday, on the evening train, and it was gone by Monday noon. (NP2)

October 6, 1916 – Several farmers were in town Wednesday to get coal out of the car, which the Farmers' union shipped in. (NP2)

January 5, 1917 – The Farmers' Union disposed of two cars of coal the first of the week. (NP2)

There were other sources, relatively nearby, where residents could go to get coal. There was coal in Red Lodge, Bear Creek, and Belfry, Montana, as well as Gebo, halfway between Worland and Thermopolis, Wyoming. Katie Brown and Fay Smith both remember getting coal from Red Lodge, though, most of the time, they went to Gebo. The trip to Red Lodge was long. It usually took about three days. The trip to Gebo wasn't as far, and Merl Fales remembers that the coal there was of a better quality. The Gebo coal was understandably more expensive, so occasionally, families would go together on a load, and someone would go pick it up, to help defray the cost. (I7) Eventually the railroad built a track to the Gebo Mine and started to produce the coal commercially, hauling it to nearby communities. (I1)

In the late summer of 1920, *The Powell Tribune* reports that Harry Peck and Earl Wilcox had taken hold of the Garland Coal Mine, also referred to as the Belcher Mine.

August 6, 1920 - The coal is of a quality similar in many respects to the Gebo coal, not that it is equal to Gebo coal, but what the miners call Gebo ash. It is much like the Red Lodge coal, at present, but will run much better as the slope goes deeper. Mr. Wilcox is anticipating a heavy run of business this fall and winter, he tells us, and he and Mr. Peck are making strenuous efforts to prepare for it. This is a Powell Valley mine that the people of Powell, Garland, and Deaver should support with enthusiasm.

This mine continued to pass through the hands of the Strand family and then to the Bloom family. Mrs. Bloom then leased the mine to Robert and Selma Duncan. Many of the Garland residents interviewed remembered when the Duncan family had the mine. They also recollected the Johnson and Honeyset Families as owners of adjacent mines on Coal Mine Hill. The Anderson, Jenkins, and Heiberg families were also mentioned in the interviews.

Merl Fales and Ethel Heimer remember the Johnson family as part owners of the Garland Coal Mine. Ethel recalls that the Malliot brothers, Joe and Will, worked with them. The Johnson family was a large one, and Merl notes, with some disappointment, that each of the girls was good looking and all were married to coal miners.

Jim Honeyset owned one of the mines. Jack VanLake told of the time Jim took him down into the mine. Jack couldn't recall what it looked like, but remembered that he wore his brand-new sheepskin coat down there. He ruined that coat by backing against the fire and burning a hole in it. (I26)

The Honeyset and Duncan mines were the last of the mines on Coal Mine Hill. Miners used carts to bring the coal out from underground. These carts were pulled by hand or by horses or mules to the loading area. When the wagons were in place, the carts were driven up under the scaffolding, where the coal was dumped into them.

Getting coal from the mine to someone's home was an adventure in itself. It usually took a full day, during the coldest part of the year. Joe Ries remembered hauling coal for Garland residents who didn't have a truck or wagon large enough to accomplish the task. (Cecilia Hendricks wrote that the rate at the mine was $2.50 and $3 per ton for the company to haul it. She also noted that the mine would take payment in honey.) (B5) When folks went to the mine to load their wagons, there was usually a line. This gave the men enough time to eat the lunches their wives had sent with them. Ethel Heimer remembers that her father had a horsehair coat that he would bundle up in to keep warm while on the coal run. She also remembers his return from the mine as he pulled into the yard with a wagonload of coal that would fill the wooden coal bin. (I14)

Lloyd Killiam tells the story of how he got his coal home one winter day.

"I was 12 or 13 when I learned to drive. Dad had an old Model T made into a pick-up, and he said, 'Now that's your car, and the responsibilities that go with that are that you have to go to the coal mine and haul coal.' It was cold. It had no top on it, just a windshield. I'd go up to the mine and fill it with coal - all I could get on it. They didn't have a paved road then; it was graveled with lots of potholes. I was coming down that hill. It was colder than hell, when I went through Garland. Old Dorothy Tule saw me. When I got to town, I just backed into the garage and started unloading coal.

Dorothy pulled her brand, new Chevy in behind me and went to my dad. She said, 'Bud, I followed that son of yours down the hill, and he was doing 60 mph with half a ton of coal on there.'

Dad just said, 'I don't know about that, but he got the coal down here.' (Dad was something else.)" (I19)

The living conditions for the families who lived and worked at the mine were pretty bad. Of the two homes next to mines, neither home had indoor plumbing. Even if they had had it, the water in the area was not good. So, after a long hard day of working in the mine they had to haul their water. (I24)

The mines on Coal Mine Hill were not safe. This factor definitely lent to their demise. The Duncan mine lost four men in the mines when a pocket of poison gasses spilled its deadly fumes into the shafts. (NP2) Both mines were also plagued by water seeping in from the Frannie Canal. Honeyset purchased a pump and tried to pump out the water but finally gave up. (I7) By the mid 1940's, both mines were closed, and, in the late 1950's, the government filled them in.

Today all that remains of those holes in the ground, that kept the Garland residents warm for 50 years, are a few pieces of lumber, some blackened earth, and the stories.

Chapter 8 - Convenience and Technology Change Everything

L ife in Garland has become much easier over the years. Not only have tractors made a huge difference in the lives of Garland's farmers, but little things we take for granted every day have made life a little better too. Since the early days of Garland, electricity, refrigerators, indoor plumbing, and telephones have become standard fare in almost every home. These are conveniences early residents didn't have. Some areas of Garland have only enjoyed these amenities for a little over 70 years. Primitive living conditions like those our forbearers accepted without question are not even a distant memory for most of us living in Wyoming today.

The people of Garland in its infancy did have a means to cool their food, but it was very different from what we have today. Outdoor icehouses stored blocks of ice for use inside the home. Most people had one of these icehouses on their own property or they shared one with a neighbor. Every winter, families had to put up ice or rely on businesses for their supply in the summer. There were two places where they could go to get ice. The gravel pit, used as a base for the new tracks, was dug in 1900 by the railroad. It filled with water and became an excellent place to get ice in the winter. In 1914, the going price for ice picked up at the gravel pit was about 50 cents per ton. However, several families chose to go to the Deaver Reservoir, 12 miles away, as the ice there was not as alkaline and cost only 25 cents per ton. (B4)

During the earliest days of Garland, John A. Thorpe, Bert Alexander, and Charley Birks supplied residents with ice.

January 30, 1906 – John A. Thorpe, our enterprising butcher, has erected a large ice house and will put up 100 tons of ice for use next summer.   (NP1)

January 30, 1906 – Bert Alexander is putting up a vast quantity of ice for Charley Birks. Mr. Birks supplied practically the whole town last year with the frozen liquid. (NP1)

February 3, 1906 – J.A. Thorpe has just completed the work of putting up 100 tons of ice in his new ice house. The quality is the best we have ever seen in these parts. Mr. Thorpe has already contracted most of it out and promises to make a nice, little wad out of his stack of frozen liquid. (NP1)

Later, an icehouse was moved to the gravel pit so that ice could be stored on the premises. Earl Jones remembers how the ice house came to be there.

"We moved one of the hotels (from Garland). My dad helped move the hotel down for an ice house inside the gravel pit. I remember Herf Graham had a team of horses, [that he used when] he cut ice. The ice was cut in chunks about a foot thick, sometimes more. They would be about 3 foot by 6 foot chunks. He had a slide there. They [the men] would push the slabs or chunks up to a slide. Then, they had a team hooked up to pull the ice up and down [it] into a wagon for whoever wanted ice. Dad used to get ice, all the time, at the icehouse. That day, they loaded the old hotel with ice and put sawdust and coal dust around it, so it would keep for the people that wanted it." (I17)

Putting up ice was something of an art form. It seems that everyone did it basically the same way, but each person had a theory of how to cut the ice and store it a little more efficiently. Ethel Heimer was impressed by Al Popien's techniques. He sawed each block by hand, and then would caulk it with snow and wood. He would get six to eight blocks together and then sit on it while the horses pulled the blocks up on planks for storage. If folks wanted a block, they could just break one off. (I14) Alden Anderson remembers watching them cut ice as a kid:

"I went up there and watched them cut the ice. They had this ice cutter. It went along and cut one strip. It had an edge, and that cutter would hang off the edge. It chipped a groove for the use of a handsaw to the ice, making the blocks even. One horse had sharp shoes on. That way, he could walk on the ice."

Families with icehouses also had their own techniques for storing ice. Some used a layer technique: a layer of ice, a layer of sawdust, a layer of ice, and so on. (I19) The Ries and Hendricks families shared an icehouse, which meant sharing the cost and labor of getting ice. They used straw, bags, and rags to insulate their ice. (I23) Jim Hart's brother built an icehouse for their family. They usually had several tons of ice, insulated by sawdust and straw. They covered the floor with sawdust, six to eight feet deep. Then, they surrounded the walls with sawdust and straw about a foot thick. When the insulation was complete, they stacked the 200-300 pound chunks in the icehouse. (I13) Why do all that work? Fay Smith gives us some refreshing reasons:

"We had a long building. It had two garages on the ends, and in the middle, was this icehouse. They [the men] cut those ice cubes about the same size and packed them in sawdust and straw. Then, in the summer we used them. We had ice cream. Mom made the best ice cream. We had real cream and all the good stuff to make it with. On occasion, we had ice water too."

Those who didn't have icehouses depended on the ice businesses in Powell and Garland. Ice could be purchased and picked up there, or it could be delivered. It was insulated with sawdust, straw, or coal slack to keep it frozen. Ice usually lasted in the icehouse until about mid-summer. (I6) However, on occasion, it could last longer. *The Powell Tribune* reported in 1916, that Claude Campbell was still delivering ice in August. Later, Mr. Daily became the ice man. He had a regular route, and the kids loved to see him come. The cost was about 25 cents per block. (I2) Herb Jones and Bonnie Hiller both remember that when he came, he would give each child a chip of ice. Bonnie's mother had a place in the cellar where she kept their block of ice wrapped up in an old comforter. She would set their cream and other items that needed to stay cold around it.

Soon indoor ice boxes became readily available. The ice man still came around in his pickup to deliver ice weekly. It was cut so that it would fit into the top cabinet. This cabinet had a pipe in it so that the water could drain out. The food was stored in the lower cabinet which was separated from the top portion. Ethel Hiemer comments on how nice it was to have the ice delivered to the house. She also remembers that when the ice man came, her mother, like Fay's, would make homemade ice cream.

Eventually, a dike was put into the gravel pit, dividing it in two smaller sections. Lloyd Killiam was disappointed by this because he says it ruined the gravel pit. People could still get ice, but the long ice skating area was ruined and the trout fishing went downhill. (I19)

Indoor plumbing, when it finally arrived on the scene, was definitely another change for the better. Can you imagine braving a winter storm to run out to the outhouse or to get water from a frozen creek? Some of the residents interviewed can, because they lived it. By the early 1920's, some people in Garland were lucky enough to have indoor plumbing, but for most, it wasn't until the late 1930's, or even the 1940's, before this "luxury" became commonplace.

In earlier chapters, it has been mentioned that some people had good water wells while others had to haul their water. Fay Smith remembers that Joe Bob Cubbage carried his water from the depot to his store by the bucket-loads. She remembers him placing one of the buckets in the store for everyone. If you needed a drink, there was a dipper near the bucket that you could use. (I25) Alden Anderson hauled his water from the Shoshone River. His family had a sled that would hold two barrels. He would load them up with water, put canvas over the barrels, and secure them down with metal hoops to keep the water from slopping out. (I1)

In the beginning, many residents didn't have "complete" plumbing. Some had pitcher pumps, or they devised some other inventive way of bringing water to the house. Fay Smith describes the house that her parents built in 1927 as having a "sort of water system." They pumped water from the river to a tank and then from the tank, via a pitcher pump, into the sink. They still had to heat the water to fill the bathtub. (I25) Bonnie Hiller appreciated their little pitcher pump:

"We always had a pitcher pump, from what I remember. I can never remember not having a pitcher pump in the kitchen. You just appreciated that little, indoor pitcher pump. If I used the one outside to pump a bucket of water, by the time I got back in, the prime was lost on the pump and you had to start all over, if you needed more water. But I miss our water - good water. We had a 15-foot well out there on the homestead. The only problem was [that] in the spring, to pump my wash water, I would have to pump it the night before and wait till morning to pump my rinse water because the pump would run out of water. When the water table rose after irrigation started, I didn't have to wait to pump my rinse water the next morning." (I15)

It took a lot of hard work to get plumbing to the houses. Merl Fales's father had a difficult time plumbing water to their house. He dug two wells that didn't work. The third did, but he had to dig it 12 to 14 feet deep, to get good water. (I7) Melvin Scott dug a half mile of water line, by hand, to his house in 1938. He tells the story with a sigh and is thankful he was a young man at the time. (I24) Herb Jones spent the entire fall of 1948 hand-digging lines to his home so his family could have indoor plumbing. (I18) The house that Jack VanLake grew up in was a "Montgomery Ward" house and had the plumbing already installed. The home just needed water plumbed to it. Jack told the story of how his father planned to get the plumbing working.

"I remember when Dad punched a well in the basement; he must have dug it in. But he was going to put half a stick of dynamite down there to help with the process. Oh boy! My mom, she just really cried and went on about how he was going to blow the house up! He didn't, you know, and we had good water right away. They had the septic tanks in, and everything was ready. That was something; I don't think anybody had septic tanks in them days. It was already built in, right in the house." (126)

Some of the holdup to getting indoor plumbing was getting electricity to the houses. It was the late 1920's to the late 1930's before Garland had electricity. Up to that point most families used kerosene or gas lamps for lighting and wood stoves for cooking. Bonnie Hiller describes life before electricity:

"You see, when I grew up, there was no electricity in the area. I think it was 1939 before we got electricity. I have really been glad that I lived through those years, that I can remember those experiences. We had our gasoline lamp. My father would pump that up, and you had the mantles, and it gave a very bright light. I know it would always hang there in the kitchen until everybody went to the living room, and then it would go with you to the living room.

And, of course, this old house had no insulation. But we had a big stove. I remember that stove in the living room. Dad would fill it up with coal, and it went all night. It kept that area warm. The bedroom doors were closed when you went to bed. We kids couldn't wait to get up in the morning and get behind that stove to get warm. I remember waking up in the mornings with the water in my glass frozen, and the bed clothes sticking to the wallpaper on the north side of my room because the frost was coming in. There was no electricity, so of course, we didn't have electric blankets, but Mother would warm up the old flat irons. She would get the flat irons hot and wrap them in newspaper and then in a towel and put them in our beds. So we got into a warm bed with those hot irons like that.

Mom - she could cook. I like to cook, but I have never had to cook where I couldn't set the temperature. She was a good cook, and she made the most beautiful angel food cakes. And I can remember, she would open that oven door and feel in there. How she knew how many sticks of wood would get the temperature she needed, I wonder. It was an art, in those days, to be able to do the things that they did. The kids tease me that I have an asbestos throat. I want things good and hot. And I think it is because of those old stoves we had in those days. The one we had was a Majestic, the cook stove. And they had a reservoir with the water on the end that kept hot water in it, but you could move things around to keep everything warm. If you had something ready before something else, you could keep it hot by putting it in the back. Everything was always warm when it was served. My mother always got everybody sat down before she brought the food to the table.

Not that it makes any difference, but that old stove in the living room had a magazine that fed the coal in. Dad would fill that magazine in that stove and set the draft so it would just feed slowly through the night and not go out. It would keep the living room and that area warm.

I can remember the coal oil stove we had. It had an oven on it that sat over the burners. Of course, that was the way we heated our flat irons. When we got done cooking, we turned an iron skillet over our flat irons, [we] put about three around the lid, then put the iron skillet over them, to hold the heat in them. Those are the kinds of things my kids just can't imagine. Like I said, I am glad that I lived through those years." (I15)

In his book, *From Beaver to Oil,* Dave Wasden talks about the fact that there were several different kinds of lighting systems. They came in all sizes and shapes. Some were mounted on the wall; some had reflectors, and some were large, with circular wicks and decorative shades. Some were used in the homes, as well as outside. He also talks about lamps that used coal oil fuel that came in five-gallon square tin cans. (B9) Ruth Hart remembered that the gasoline lamps her parents had were filled from underneath the pressure tank below the lamp. The mantles that went with the lamp were one and a half to two inches long and stretched around circular tubing. That tank was pumped and pressured up and would burn with a bright, white light. (I13) Fay Smith remembers having a carbide system before her father bought a 32-volt generator. It came with batteries and an entire electrical system, so her family had lights and a 32-volt refrigerator. Vern Fales remembered their gas lights but also the battery-operated radio:

"Dad had a battery radio. Well, once in awhile we would talk him into letting us listen to it at night, but most of the time, it was news. The news came on, and when the news was over, it was off. He didn't want to buy the batteries." (I8)

The Powell Flat was the first to get electricity, but Garland wasn't far behind. Jim Hart's father, F.G. Hart, and Bob Allen were instrumental in getting the ball rolling. With the Rural Electrification Act passed, funds were made available for cooperatives to be formed and organized to distribute electricity to various farm areas. F.G. Hart and Bob Allen got an interested group of individuals together and formed the Garland Light and Power Company. The company officially started bringing electricity to the rural areas around Garland in 1937. (I13) Today, it is still going strong and supplying energy to power the computer used to write this book.

Telephone technologies have changed tremendously over the years since they were first introduced in Garland. The technology has gone from crank phones and "Hello Girls" to cell phones. The first recorded telephone line into the Bighorn Basin came in 1899. The lines were run by the Red Lodge and Wyoming Telephone Company. The line went from Red Lodge, past Eagles' Nest, to Cody, to Meeteetse, to Greybull, and on to Basin. Telephone exchanges were built in Basin, Meeteetse, and Cody. In 1903, the exchanges were bought by the Rocky Mountain Bell Telephone Company. Later that year, they had three crews working on three new lines. One crew worked north from Thermopolis. One worked from Cody to Meeteetse, and the third worked from Bridger to Frannie and through Garland to Penrose. At Penrose, the line branched and went to Byron and Lovell, with a sub-branch to Cowley. The three main lines came together in Burlington. (B9) But now this did not mean that every home had a phone. In those days, only a select few businesses had them. Phones were installed in the Garland Mercantile, John J. Simmons Store in Byron, the Crosby Mercantile in Cowley, and Frank Strong's hotel in Lovell. By paying a toll charge, it was possible to communicate

A crew building telephone lines between Basin and Garland, Wyoming. Photo courtesy of Fred Lang.

directly with a number of distant towns. By the end of 1903, there were fewer than 100 telephones in the Bighorn Basin. (B9) By 1906, however, many of the Garland businesses had their own lines.

June 30, 1906 – Telephone Exchange – Following is a list of the local exchange telephone subscribers installed this week:

> The Guard Office {Central}
> Garland Merchantile Co.
> B&M Agent {Depot}
> Garland Hardware and Lumber Co.
> Schwoob and Reynolds {Livery Barn}
> Gate City Hotel
> Thos. Long residence
> A. Jones, Gen'l Merchant
> Chas. Burke, Saloon
> Lee Saloon (NP1)

Soon, small country lines organized exchange services that were financed by the settlers. The exchange offices usually had two operators - a day operator, who worked ten hours, and a night operator, who worked 14. They were paid $30 per month and were known as the "Hello Girls" or the "Jingle Sisters." These girls knew everything that was going on in the community.

The people of Garland could not wait to be part of the telephone trend. *The Garland Guard* was part of the push for the telephone system and enthusiastically promoted the soon-to-be-operational telephone exchange.

January 6, 1906 – *Hello Central! Prominent Garland Men Working for Local Telephone Exchange. It Will Soon be Installed Here.* Some of Garland's enterprising businessmen, headed by that progressive, wide awake pusher, Thomas Long, of the Garland Mercantile Company, are exceedingly busy working up a local telephone exchange for Garland. Enough instruments have already been spoken for to make the exchange a certainty, and it only remains for the Bell Company to get busy and see that the exchange is installed.

Mr. Long has personally taken the matter up with Manager Frisby, and the latter has given impetus to the movement by his assurance that the exchange is to be put in as soon as Superintendent Vanca arrives, and he is expected within a few days.

But this is not all. The towns of Byron, Cowley, and Lovell are to be taken into the same exchange. These towns are building up with remarkable rapidity, and a four-town exchange has become an absolute necessity.

The town of Garland has increased in population from a paltry few hundred to nearly the one thousand mark during the past six months, and it is no stretch of the imagination to predict that by the first of January, 1907, its population will number two thousand.

Several prominent Cody merchants are going to erect branch stores here in the near future. Business is brisk, and the sun of prosperity is shining for all who have money to invest here. The work of constructing the Corbett Tunnel has begun, and within a short time work on the canal, is to commence, and then, that great body of land known as the Garland Flat will be thrown open for entry, with the results that hundreds of settlers will locate in and around Garland. The onward march to those favored lands will be something immense when once begun. Watch for it.

But to return to our telephone subject. It is perhaps not generally known that Lovell has an independent telephone system. The owners of this independent line, it is learned, intend to extend their line to Cowley and also to Byron, and it is to head off this movement that is causing the Bell Company to get busy in this section.

The writer has the personal assurance of Mgr. Frisby that this four-town exchange will be installed. However, to Mr. Long belongs the credit of opening negotiations with Manager J.F. Frisby, looking to the installation of the proposed exchange.

This is an important step in the way of progress and will lead to many other of equal importance. The next move will be to incorporate the town. Shake off the swaddling clothes which are getting too small for us, and put on the remnants of genuine progressiveness. Boost for the telephone exchange. (NP1)

January 6, 1906 – Get in your order for a telephone for the new exchange, and thereby, show the promoters that you are progressive and up to date. (NP1)

January 6, 1906 – Get onto the band wagon and boost for the Garland-Byron-Cowley-Lovell telephone exchange. It's up to us to see it's a go. (NP1)

January 13, 1906 – Do it now. Get a telephone. (NP1)

January 13, 1906 – Just get a phone now while you think of it. It will avoid the rush a little later on. (NP1)

The community newspaper, *The Garland Guard,* dutifully continued to keep its readers informed of the progress being made on the telephone exchange. In February, Manager Frisby of the Bell Phone Company was in Garland, assuring the citizens that the materials for the Garland telephone exchange would arrive shortly, and work on the exchange would begin. By June, Carl Wilson was putting in the local telephone exchange in *The Garland Guard* office. (NP1)

In 1911, Mountain States Telephone Company was organized and started to take over the exchanges owned by the Rocky Mountain States Telephone Company. In 1913, Mountain States was running the services from Basin to Worland, and in 1916, it added Garland. (B9) By this time, the lines were already in need of some repairs.

June 16, 1916 – The Mountain State Telephone Co. is repairing the line at this place. (NP2)

November 24, 1916 – A large crew of telephone men are camped near town. They are putting in new poles and stringing a line of copper wire. (NP2)

By December of 1916, a new building had been purchased to become the telephone exchange office. *The Powell Tribune* reported that there would be three "Hello Girls" instead of one. In January of 1917, it reported that the installations of the telephone fixtures were nearing completion and announced only two names to become the new "Hello Girls." Miss Mary Smith and Miss Anderson would be the operators at the new exchange in Garland. (NP2) In later years, Fay Smith remembers that May Daily was the telephone operator in Garland and that people would go into the small telephone office next to the post office to make long distance calls. (I25)

Today, the telephone system is run by computers and satellites, but in the early years, it was a very simple operation. When a call was made it would ring the operator sitting at the switchboard. The caller would tell the operator who they wanted to talk with and maybe their short three to four-digit telephone number. The operator would then connect the caller. (I6) This was not a closed system. Several families, sometimes up to 15, were on the same line. It was called a "party line." The phone would ring a certain number of times, indicating which family the call was for. For example, Ruth

Hart remembered her phone number was three short rings. Katie Brown remembers hers as being one long and three short rings, just the opposite of Melvin Scott's three longs and a short. Everyone was supposed to respect their neighbors' private calls, but occasionally, someone would "rubber," or listen in. On certain occasions, this was accepted. For instance, if the phone rang five times, it was the signal for everybody to listen for general news, meeting times, or emergency information. (I14) Melvin Scott remembers when the five-ring system was used to inform everyone that some fresh lugs of peaches had arrived in town. (I24)

The exchange office was located on the east side of Main Street, close to the post office building. (I13) Ethel Heimer thinks the exchange was in Garland until about 1938. It was then moved to Powell. Martha Jones worked as a "Hello Girl" in the Powell office during 1942 and 1943. She remembered pulling the cords out of the base and putting them into the mated receptacles for the lines of the phones the callers were trying to reach. She worked that job at night and went to school during the day. She remembered that when the doctors would go out of town, the exchange was informed where they would be. "It worked kind of like a dispatch service," Martha said with a smile. "I had my finger on the pulse of the community, at all times." (I8)

One last piece of technology, that was a big convenience to a few of the Garland homeowners, was the early, pre-fabricated home, also referred to as the Montgomery Ward House. Customers could order a home from the catalogue, choosing the floor plan they preferred. The house was then assembled, numbered, unassembled, and sent on the railroad. The customer would take his wagon down to the railroad, pick up the materials, go back to his land and start to assemble his new home. All of the pieces were pre-cut and numbered, with the family name on the lumber. It was like putting together a giant puzzle, with plumbing, wiring, and windows. The Cubbage's house, the Franklin's house, the Honey Hill house, and the house Jack VanLake grew up in are all Montgomery Ward houses. Darwin Franklin remembers that when he was changing out the window casings in their house and during other remodeling projects, that he found boards addressed to "Starr." Originally, the house had belonged to the VanEmmens, but they were related to the Starr family who had ordered and built the Cubbage's house. (I9) They probably ordered their homes at about the same time and had similar floor plans. However, after several remodeling, those layouts are very different now. Jack VanLake remembered interesting details of his Montgomery Ward Home:

We had plumbing and electricity already in it, so when they got electricity in Garland, all we had to do was hook into it. We had electricity before anybody [else] because our house was all wired, and we didn't have to do anything. The wiring all seemed right - and the plumbing - Dad punched the well in the basement, and we had water through the house right away too. The septic tank was all in [also]. I slept upstairs. The house had a wood stove down below, and the pipe kind of went up by the staircase, and in the winter time, the folks would shut that staircase and like to freeze me out up there. They didn't want all the heat to go up. We had cold, cold weather. It [the house] had a vent in the floor; they had evidently had a furnace in the basement, but it kept getting water in it and ruined the furnace. The bathroom was right behind the kitchen, in another room and they heated the hot water tank from pipes that kind of ran into the stove. It [the house] had a tub and everything in it already. (I26)

Technology has come a long way for Garland. Most residents now have satellite TV, cell phones, and computers. The only thing that hasn't made its way to Garland is high speed internet, but that is sure to arrive soon. So next time the power goes out, or your pipes freeze, or your cell phone drops a call, instead of being frustrated, think about how far we have come in just a few short decades. The 1940's were not that long ago, and it wasn't until then that most homes in Garland had the conveniences we take for granted today.

Chapter 9 - Community: Working and Playing Together

Several times throughout this book, the "community" of Garland is referred to. It was a community, in the true sense of the word. These people worked, studied, and played together. No one batted an eye when it came to helping out a neighbor. The community had sports teams, clubs, schools, churches, parties, and entertainment to keep them coming together. Ethel Heimer says it best:

"I enjoyed the Garland community because it was a close knit organization, a fun family. We just had a lot of fun together. We went to school here. We went to programs and church. We had potluck supers and pie socials." (I14)

Schools and churches tend to give communities foundations. It is hard to exclude oneself from the community if you have a child attending school or if you go to church. In the beginning, having a school in Garland was really a community effort. From 1901 until 1903, school was held in the lumber yard office. In 1903, Miss G. McQueen was the teacher, and the school year was three months long. In this same year, Garland was designated as School District #37. In 1904, school was held in the storeroom of the general store. (I16) The next year, Brown's Hall had the honors. (NA7) In May of 1905, at the annual school board meeting, a vote was passed for a special tax of 5 mills for the purpose of building a schoolhouse. D.L. Sigmon, contractor and builder, began construction of the building that summer, with the help of Tom Hopkin. It was completed in October of 1905. *The Garland Guard* complimented Sigmon as being "the best carpenter that has ever been in this section." The school year began in late October that year. The teacher was paid a salary of $50 per month. The first and last day of the school year (1905/06) was recorded in *The Garland Guard*.

October 28, 1905 – The District School began on Monday with Miss Marie Healey as principal and a fair attendance of pupils. Miss Healey, though stern in her demand for good order in the school room, is very popular with the children and has already won their love, esteem, and confidence. The children tell us that she has a very winsome disposition and quickly makes friends. That this district has secured the services of Miss Healey is a matter of which the trustees, in particular, and people, in general, ought to congratulate themselves. We predict that our school will be decidedly successful, and we urge the people to be sure and send the children to school. (NP1)

June 30, 1906 – Garland School Closes (Written by Miss Melba Adams)
Friday was the 22nd and also marked the close of the Garland School Dist. No. 37. Work from each grade was made ready for the state exhibit, which is to be at Douglas this year.

After this, the books were laid away and the morning work completed. Then the seats were removed, and everyone prepared for a good time. Dinner was served at 12, as each pupil had brought something for the dinner, which was served on a large table that extended the length of the school room and was temptingly arranged. The afternoon was pleasantly spent playing various games. The visitors present were: Mrs. R.E. Naylor, Misses M.L. McCollock, Zada Norton, Flora Wheeler, and Blanch Hurst; also Vernon King. The pupils for the term were as follows: Dwight King, Edith Reusch, May and Ola Norton, Flossie, Edith, Thurman and Leonard Hurst, Earl Holdman, Bessie and Vera Bishop, Harold, Cornelius, and Edith Denny, Norris, Tom, and Melba Adams. (NP1)

By 1908, Powell had enough people settled in and around it that there was a need for a school in Powell. So the mill levy was increased to 8 mills in order to provide for an additional school. In 1911, Park County was organized. Powell and Garland were no longer part of Big Horn County and School District #37 became School District #1, in the new county. Soon, Powell became dissatisfied with the services offered by District #1 and formed District #2. (MA&P 9) School District #1 was made up of the Garland, Penrose, Starr, and Kinne schools. By 1915, District #1 schools were doing well, with the exception of one week in February, when the schools were closed because there were several cases of scarlet fever in the Garland vicinity. *The Powell Tribune* under "Garland Items" reported the successes of District #1:

February 5, 1915 – Our school is progressing nicely. The high school students have completed some of their studies and succeeded in passing the final examination. The last step has been made and our high school is now accredited. We have the proper number of studies, our recitation periods are the required length, and now, the school board has granted us an extra month, making our school term nine months. Our high school is small, but it is certainly doing splendid work, under the skillful management of Mr. Watterman and Mr. Richards. Those in the first graduation class will be Mary Smith, Thura Campbell, Jerd Smith, and Earl Campbell. (NP2)

In May of 1915, the school year was coming to an end. The grammar and primary schools were finished, and the high school still had two weeks of cramming for exams to go. A call was made for the election of new school board members. The board needed three people to serve three-year terms. One would represent the Garland school, one the Penrose School, and one the Starr and Kinne schools. (B5) While adults were running for the school board, the students were electing their student council. On May 14, *The Powell Tribune* had two articles reporting on the results of the student council election, the progress of the past year, and hopes for the following one.

May 14, 1915 – The classes have all elected their officers. Those of the sophomores are - President, Constance Atkins; Secretary, George Cline; Treasurer, Hill Campbell; Colors - light green and white. Juniors – Thura Campbell, President; Jerd Smith, Secretary and Treasurer. Colors - maize and sky blue. (NP2)

May 14, 1915 – The teachers have been hired for this district for the coming year at Garland. The teachers are Prof. W.R. Watterman; E.D. Richards, who will be the principal; Intermediate - Miss Alta Claftin; Primary - Miss Alma VanEman. At the Starr … We have great hopes of our high school. We will not have a graduating class this year but will have one next year. We have

Garland School girls: 1. Dora Wheeler 2. Fabolia Spielman 3. Kathleen Rottinghaus
4. Lorene Miller 5. Helen Glass 6. Juanita Rottinghaus 7. Zola Bogart 8. Marjorie Early
9. Geneve VanWagner 10. Loretta 11. Dora Belle Early 12. Anna Marie Rotting
13. Bonnie Brown 14. Lydia Layman 15. Kathryn Meyers. Photo courtesy of Katie Brown.

worked hard this winter and have been recognized by the University of Wyoming and have been placed on the 3-year accredited list. Next year, we will be placed upon the 4-year list, and any students graduating from high school here can enter the University of Wyoming, without having to take extra exams. Our school is an organized body of hard workers. The president is Earl Campbell - secretary, Nava Starr; treasurer, Mary Smith. School colors - purple and gold. Motto: "Through trial to triumph." (NP2)

The 1915/16 and 1916/17 school years went by without much notice. Teachers encouraged the students to work harder to get grades up, and a new belfry was added to the school in March of 1916. In May of 1916, *The Powell Tribune* reported that the school closed with "a creditable year behind it." (NP2)

The 1917/18 school year was filled with controversy. On a national level, the United States entered World War I. Patriotism and propaganda promoting hatred of Germany was high. As a patriotic gesture supporting the German language had not been taught in the Garland schools since 1916. However, there was a healthy population of families of German descent residing in the Garland area, and this caused some tension in the community.

October 19, 1917 – An investigation has been started to ascertain the authors or author of two letters received by two young men of this community, in which their lives were threatened. No cause is given in the letter for these threats, and it is assumed that it is some pro-German, since both of these young men are intensely patriotic, as they have shown, on different occasions, by going to extremes. (NP2)

In May of 1918, some of the Garland students got it in to their heads to burn all of the German textbooks and any other German books they could find in the school. The students approached Mrs. Richards, a teacher, about their plan to burn the books. Mrs. Richards explained to them that the books belonged to and were supplied by the school board. She told them that if they went to the school board and received permission, they could have a celebration, burning the books. Mr. Richards, the principal, agreed. However, three of the older boys, two of whom were known trouble makers, didn't want to wait to hear from the school board, so they proceeded to the library during recess. They got the books, took them out on the fire escape, set

Merl Fales with two girls in front of the school. Photo courtesy of Irma Yonts.

them on fire, and began throwing the burning books down where the children played on the playground. Mr. Richards stopped them and expelled the boys until they made things right with the school board. (B5) This still did not dissuade the students and some of the community members. Pete Wood's grandfather, Mr. Woods, was the janitor at the school at the time. Pete said that his grandfather had always felt kind of responsible for what happened next. Whether he did it on purpose or accidentally only history can rightly say, but he left the front door of the schoolhouse unlocked one afternoon. (I27) That evening, a mob of seven men grabbed Mr. Richards and made him go with them to the schoolhouse. He didn't want to go because he had signed a contract to protect school property, but he was forced to do so. When they arrived at the school, a crowd had gathered. No one knew that Mr. Richards was there against his will. He was kept there until most of the German books had been burned, and then he was taken home. (B5) Not all of the German books were destroyed, however. The Starr family, of German descent, had hidden several books, by taking them into their attic and dropping them down the walls. The Cubbages found them, in later years, when they were remodeling the house. (I6)

Garland school and the student body. Photo courtesy of Norman "Pete" Woods.

During the next couple of years, school attendance numbers in District #1 were dwindling, and the number in District #2 were on the rise. In 1922, the two districts were consolidated to become District #1 of Park County. In that same year, the Garland and Powell High Schools were also consolidated leaving Garland with only primary classes. In 1931, all classes were consolidated into Powell. (NA6)

There were three school buildings in Garland over the years. The first, built by Ted Hopkin and D.L. Sigmon, was a clapboard building with a bell tower and a stage for performances. This building has since been moved onto a local farm and is being used as a barn. The bell tower has been removed. The next school was a log building. It has been moved several times, for different purposes. It was eventually moved to Powell and became the Chamber of Commerce building. It was moved once more and is now a residence. (I21) The third is the building that today is known as the Garland Church. This is where many of the residents interviewed went to grade school. Some went to high school in Garland as well, but many graduated from Powell after the schools were consolidated.

The third schoolhouse was a two-story building heated by a portable gas heating stove. The two floors separated the grade school from the high school. There were eight school rooms; each was adequate for about two grades. The high school classes were held upstairs in the two classrooms on the south side of the school. The principal's office was also on the upper floor. The other eight grades were predominately in the lower rooms, to keep the younger kids from climbing the stairs. (I13) After the high school consolidated with Powell, the first through fourth grades were in the classrooms downstairs and the fifth through eighth grade classes were upstairs. The first and second grade classrooms were on the south side of the school. The third and fourth grade classrooms were on the north side. (I9) (The floor plan for the upstairs is not clear.) There was also a library and an eating area. (I13)

Pete Woods and Earl Jones remember stories from their childhood about the way students were kept in line at the Garland School. (At times, the teachers were disciplining students close to their own age.)

"We had a Russian kid in our class. He was a big, strong kid, and one of the teachers went after him. Paul Wagner, I think was his name. The teacher had a blackboard pointer in her hand. Paul was kind of a big guy, older and not doing his school work. She whacked him over the head with the pointer. I can still hear old Paul yell, 'You better watch out.' He didn't follow through on the threat but might have intimidated the teacher some. (I27)

Uncle Bud (Boyd Jones) told me that one of the superintendents or teachers at the school had a rubber hose to paddle the kids with when they were bad. So they sneaked into the school one night and filled the hose with water, putting a cork on each end. One of the boys was going to do something [the next day] so that the teacher would have to whip him; that cork would come out and spray water all over the school. That night the hose froze. The next day, as planned, the boy misbehaved and the teacher whipped him with the frozen rubber hose. It didn't turn out as funny as they had thought. (I17)

There were several different teachers who taught in Garland over the years. Besides the ones mentioned in the previous newspaper articles, the following are names the residents interviewed remembered: John Schell, Mrs. Lord, Mrs. A.O. Crane, Mrs. Powers, and Ethel Phillips. (Ethel Phillips married Pete Wood, so many residents remember her as Ethel Wood.) Bonnie Hiller recollects that Ethel taught the fifth grade. She was a gym teacher as well and even taught the students how to dance. Bonnie also remembers Mr. Will. He was the janitor and rang the school bell. She says that he was "awfully handy."
"

If you had a broken shoestring or anything else happened, you went to Mr. Will. Once a year, Mr. Will had his treat time and in those days, candy or anything like it was a real treat. You never knew when he was going to do it, and you never knew which room he was going to start in. But we knew when it happened. If it didn't start in your room, and you happened to be under the room up above [the one] that he started in, you could hear this stuff hitting the floor. It would be like wrapped kisses and things like that. But he would walk into the room, with a laugh, and start throwing candy. And he did this once a year. He was an institution himself. He was the kindest person. He was the janitor and kept the furnace going. And he would just do anything a kid would need, if you needed something fixed. And I'm sure he was that way for the teachers too. He was just one of those people that was an institution in himself, that you just never forget." (I15)

Getting to school was a challenge. If students lived too far from the school, their parents may have rented a place, or had their children stay with friends and family in town during the school week. Other students came to school by wagon, by sleigh in the winter, or by bus, in later years. Some students walked or rode horses. The children at Mantua rode the train in on Monday, stayed in town until Friday, and then rode the train home. (I16) Donald (JP) Ries, Joe Ries' father, drove a converted sheep wagon with a canvas top. He picked up the kids as he drove to town. (I23) In 1917, Fleming Kilgore and Henry Meyers were hired by the school board to drive school wagons. (NP1) Katie Brown and Ethel Heimer both remember their dad, Henry Meyers, hauling kids to school. They remember him taking the wagon box, putting it on skids, and gathering the kids up for school, when the snow was too deep to drive the school wagon.

"I can remember that Dad drove the school wagon, and he had a team of horses hooked to the sled. He took us to school on the sled. Momma had a black fox muff, and I got to wear her muff. (I2)

We would go through the fields and bypass the roads that were closed. We thought that was quite exciting. We would take blankets and really enjoy it. It seemed like a long ways. It was only 2 1/2 miles, but it seemed like a long, long way for us to go on the wagon." (I14)

After the schools were consolidated, Charley Cooley drove the bus that picked up the kids in Penrose. Alden Anderson remembers the bus as one Charley had fixed up, with a row of seats down the middle and a seat around on the outside of each row. Charley hauled about 20 or 25 kids from the Penrose area to Powell. (I1)Charley Peterson was Bonnie Hiller's bus driver when she went to Powell. (I15)

If you ask any student what their favorite part of school is, most of them will say recess. The residents of Garland would agree. Many of them have fond memories of the games they played on the school playground. Sometimes, the teachers would even play with them. The playground equipment consisted of a merry-go-round, a teeter totter, and swings. The Garland children played many of the same games as we might see now on the playground, games like Hide and Seek, Kick the Can, Red Rover, basketball, baseball, and Marbles. (There was once even a playground wedding. Jack Lewis was the groom, and Mary VanWagoner the bride. Darwin Franklin was the best man, and Emma Johnson the bridesmaid.) (I9) Two games that are not commonly played today that were played on the Garland playground were Pump Pump Pull Away and Fox and Geese. Pump Pump Pull Away was a tug-o'-war game. It consisted of two teams, one on each side of the rope. A line was drawn on the ground in the middle. Then someone would yell, "Pump, Pump, Pull away. If you don't come, I'll pull you away." The team that pulled the other team across the line first won. (I14) Fox and Geese was a winter game of tag. A large outer circle was drawn in the snow, and a smaller one was drawn in the middle of it. The center circle was "home." The game started with one or two "foxes" that were trying to catch the "geese" as they left home. Once a fox tagged a goose, the goose became a fox, until there were no more geese. (I1)

The Garland School also sponsored several programs that entertained the community. Programs were for entertainment and civic purposes. Some school programs coincided with church programs. The Christmas program of 1905, organized by Miss Marie Healy was covered by *The Garland Guard* in great detail. Everyone was invited, and all who wanted to could bring a present to put on the Christmas tree for the children.

December 30, 1905 – *Christmas Program* The district school of Garland, under the very able and efficient management of Miss Marie Healy, assisted by that good and untiring friend of the little ones, Mrs. Mary McColloch, did itself exceedingly proud with its excellent entertainment Christmas night at the new school house.

The room was tastefully decorated throughout. Immediately over the stage was the inscription, "Welcome" in large, even letters, while in the center of the room, suspended on beautiful scallops, were two lovely, silver, Christmas bells. On the north side of the room were the words "A Happy New Year" while on the south, were the words, "Merry Christmas." On the stage was the beautiful Christmas tree, supplied to the school by Rulon Robison, who made a trip into the hills to get it. This was also tastefully decorated and decked with toys, dolls, fancy boxes, and picture books in profusion.

The following program was carried out, much to the delight and entertainment of the large number of people present. Each number was warmly encored, and all who took part acquitted themselves admirably. James F. Jensen's impersonation of Santa Claus was perfect. Great credit is due Misses Healey and McCulloch for their splendid achievements in the excellent arrangement of the affair and in the manner in which the pupils were trained in so short a time.

Song	"Merry Christmas Bells," By School
Recitation	"Christmas Wishes"
Recitation	"The Christmas Stocking," May Norton
Song	"Christmas Hymn"
Recitation	"A Letter to Santa," Thurman Hurst
Recitation	"Why Santa Laughed," Russell Denney
Song	"Christmas Bell," By School
Dialogue	"Mr. St. Nicholas," Vernon King and pupils of the School
Recitation	"The Day of Days," Lila Crandall
Recitation	"The Quarrel," Edith Denney
Song	"He Loved Us So," Misses Healey and McCullock, and Messrs. Jensen and King
Recitation	"Just Before Christmas," Dwight King
Recitation	"Christmas Helpers," Edith Hurst
Recitation	"Christmas Questions," Jess Vaterlaus
Song	"Shine Out O Blessed Star," By School
Recitation	"A Christmas Thought," Flossie Hurst
Drill	"Christmas Stars," Lila Crandall, Flossie Hurst, May Norton, Edith Hurst, Ola Norton, Edith Denney, May Vaterlaus
Recitation	"A Catastrophe," Cornelius Denney
Recitation	"Little Helpers," Lawrence States
Song	"We've Brought in our Stockings," Pupils of the School, mixed voices
Song	"Santa Claus," James Fedensen
Song	"Santa's Welcome," By School

"Merry Christmas to all and to all a good night"

It is no exaggeration to state that this entertainment was the best that has ever been given in Garland, and more of this kind of entertainment should be had. (NP1)

Being community oriented, administrators and teachers saw to it that some of the school programs were centered on civic projects. The following are three of the many special programs presented to or by the school: In March of 1916, the school board sponsored a contest to let the students design the school grounds. The agriculture class measured the school grounds. Then each student came up with a plan for the landscaping, including fences, trees, and lawn. At the time, there were rumors of a tennis court, but that never came to pass. Hill Campbell received first place for his plans. (NP2) In December of 1917, Mrs. F.A. Mills gave a talk about "The Needs of the Children in the War Zone" to the Junior Red Cross Society, organized by the school. And in February of 1918, Miss Underwood, County Superintendent of Schools, presented information to the students and their parents about the importance of buying Thrift and War Saving Stamps. (NP2)

High school graduation ceremonies were presented in the community by both the school and the Methodist Church.

May 5, 1916 – The Juniors and Seniors decorated the church house Tuesday and Wednesday; the decorations were in Senior class colors, sky blue and maize, and the class flower was pink carnations. Rev. Stephenson, of Cody, came down Saturday to deliver the Baccalaureate sermon, Sunday evening. The program was composed of music, by the chorus, and the address. The Senior Class considered itself lucky in securing the services of such an able man. – A large delegation from Powell attended the commencement exercises Wednesday evening. – The graduating exercises of Garland High School took place Wednesday evening at the M.E. Church, and the program published in *The Tribune* last week was very creditably rendered throughout. (NP2)

April 27, 1917 – The Baccalaureate sermon for the Senior Class of Garland High School will be delivered in the Methodist Church, Sunday evening, by Rev. W.H. Clark, of Billings. – Commencement exercises of the graduating class will be held in the Methodist Church, Thursday night May 3rd. Judge Percy W. Metz, of Basin, will be the speaker of the evening. – The members of the high school were royally entertained at the schoolhouse Thursday night by the high school faculty. (NP2)

After the schools consolidated, the two-story schoolhouse became a community center. It soon was the heart of Garland. Elections were, and still are, held there. There were also many big dinner celebrations in the old building. The men pitched horseshoes, while the women prepared the meal. Then, card parties became popular. (I7) Most fondly remembered were the dances held there. On Saturday evenings, during the winter, everyone for miles around, came to the dances at the old schoolhouse. It was fun for the whole family. Sometimes the dances would be to support a cause like the Red Cross Society, and sometimes it would be just for the fun of it. Each family brought something for the potluck dinner, sandwiches mostly but some cakes and pies. Every week, a different family would make the coffee. The men played cards, while the women got dinner together and put the babies to sleep. Two tables were pushed together in the coat room. The coats were piled on the tables, and then the sleeping babies were placed on the coats. The dancing took place upstairs in what was turned into a community hall. Warren Cubbage described it as a big, huge, open room. The furnace vents went up through the center of the room but were designed to look like support pillars. He remembered big,

The Garland church and congregation. Possibly 1927. Photo courtesy of Norman "Pete" Woods

wide stairs that led up to the dance floor. (I6) Bonnie Hiller recalls that Jim Erwin, a WWI veteran, played the piano. Earl Jones remembers that Merlin Glass called the square dances and Herb Jones says that his father and Hazel Clark sang. Katie Brown describes the dances best:

"It was the most wonderful thing, when the whole community came in. We ate, played cards, and danced, and put the babies to sleep."

There were a couple of church organizations in Garland, but the majority of the citizens seemed to be of the Methodist persuasion. Today, we talk about keeping church and state separate, but in Garland, they were very much a part of each other. As seen previously, graduation ceremonies were a joint effort, as were many of the plays. The first church services were held in the schoolhouse and were conducted by a Methodist pastor, Rev. Clark. On alternating Sundays, the Baptist pastor, Rev. Olmstead, conducted services. Olmstead was a homesteader, and Clark was a bank clerk. (NA7) Rev. C.E. Fenton, of Basin, and Rev. Givin of York, Nebraska, were also invited to conduct services in Garland. (NP1) A little, white church was built north of the railroad tracks, across from where the Garland Church stands today. While staffed by the Methodists, this was a non-denominational, community church. Rev. Clark held Sunday services there. After Rev. Clark left, the church did not have enough money to keep a pastor regularly employed, so on occasion, the pastor from Deaver would hold services at the church. If he wasn't available, local people would give the sermon. Preacher Weiry and Judge Campbell were two of the memorable locals. It is said that Judge Campbell gave a pretty good sermon because he had a pair of mules he spent the whole week cursing. (I19) Katie Brown remembers that the church was a big part of the community. Many of the children were baptized there and it was the place where the community prayed for sick children, performed and enjoyed plays, and held their funeral and wedding services.

"And we used to have the best times in the church because that is where the children from school did their performances. Once I was Topsie in *Uncle Tom's Cabin*. My mom blackened me with burned cork - my face and neck and hands and hair - because I had to look good for *Uncle Tom's Cabin*. And I didn't get completely white again for a month, and it took a lot of scrubbing. But we would have our plays and our funerals [there]. Everything was in the little church. And it didn't make any difference what denomination you were; you just went to the Garland Church." (I2)

A few residents remembered Easter Sunrise Services, held on top of the coal mine. For several years, on Easter Sunday, Garland residents would wake up before the sun and make their way to Coal Mine Hill by foot, horse, or vehicle. A cross was placed at a high spot in the hills, east of where the highway runs today. They would congregate at the cross and wait for the sun to rise. At sunrise, the Easter sermon would be given. After services were over, some people made their way back home while others stayed and enjoyed the hills for the rest of the day.

School, community, and church activities kept the people of Garland pretty busy, but if they wanted something different, it wasn't hard to find. From the very beginning, the people of Garland found and hosted a variety of entertainment opportunities. The railroad brought with it several traveling troupes that would play nightly at each stop. (B9) Many of the performances and parties were held at Brown's Hall, or the Opera House, or the Methodist Church. (These may have all been the same building.) The early residents had plenty of entertainment to choose from.

There were balls:

September 22, 1905 – E.A. Kelly will give a Grand Ball and Oyster Supper next Friday night in the Crystal Saloon building which he is now fixing up for a hotel. He has secured good music for the occasion, and the spacious floor will be in fine condition. During the dance, refreshments will be provided, such as ice cream, cake, coffee, and soft drinks. A special invitation is extended to the young people of Byron and vicinity. A swell time is assured all who attend the "Harvest Dance." (NP1)

January 27, 1906 – A very pleasant dance was given Tuesday night, in the dining room of the Gate City Hotel, which was largely attended. These parties are becoming very popular, and it is to be hoped that they will be kept up periodically during the winter months. Mr. and Mrs. Dural Campman furnished excellent music for the occasion. (NP1)

February 7, 1906 – A Basket Ball will be given on the evening of Washington's Birthday, next Thursday, at the Gate City Hotel. The Ladies will please bring baskets containing supper for two, which will be sold at auction to the highest bidder, the proceeds to be used for the benefit of the school. All are cordially invited. (NP1)

March 3, 1906 – The Basket Ball given at the Gate City Hotel, on the evening of Washington's Birthday, was a most successful affair, from any point of view. Over $35 was realized from the auction sale of baskets, which is for the benefit of the school. (NP1)

There were moving picture shows:

May 5, 1905 – *Return Engagement – Edmundson's Magical and Moving Picture Show - Set for Thursday, May 11th.* Mr. Edmundson writes *The Guard,* from Otto, that he will play a return date program. *The Destruction of Martinique* will be reproduced in moving scenes, showing a panoramic view of Mt. Pelee Volcano in action, the taking out of the dead and wounded, etc. [There will be] new, comic scenes for the children and a mechanical opera of "Joan of Arc," as produced at Drury Lane, London. This is one of the finest moving scenes ever photographed. Also [included] is the great Corbett fight show, the knockout blow. A dance will be given after the show. The above program, including the dance, will also be given at Lovell, May 10th. This is one of Mr. Edmundson's best programs, and we predict for him a full house. (NP1)

May 12, 1905 – T.E. Edmundson, the "Yankee Wizard," concluded a very successful showing tour of the Basin here last night. The program was a most superb one, the moving scenes taking the house by storm. Mr. Edmundson was everywhere greeted with large and enthusiastic crowds. During his tour of the county, Mrs. Edmundson remained at Garland, at the Hopkin Hotel, and during her brief stay here, has made many warm friends. Their home is in Seattle, Wash. (NP1)

June 9, 1905 – An entire new program will be presented Tuesday night by the Moore Concert Co. No one can afford to miss it. Remember the dates - Good times for all at popular prices. – Don't overlook the dates set for the return of Moore's Concert Company, [at] Brown's Hall, Tuesday, June 20th. Popular prices. – New and exciting moving picture scenes; new program; new musical selections by the celebrated Moore Concert Company – Tuesday, June 20. – Most everybody wants to see *The Great Train Robbery* reproduced by Moore's celebrated moving picture machine. And it's worth going many miles to see. Brown's Hall, June 20th. (NP1)

June 23, 1905 – The Moore's Concert Company played return engagements here Tuesday and Wednesday evenings. This company has given such a fine, high-class entertainment that their return engagements are eagerly looked for wherever they have held forth. This cultured and refined company will play two more engagements in Cody on the nights of July 4th and 5th. They will be greeted with a packed house, which they justly deserve. They hold forth at Arnold's Hall. (NP1)

There were a variety of performances - comedic, musical, and magical:

May 19, 1905 – Congo Twins and their company. The ideal colored artists, singers, dancers, acrobats. The world's best gun and baton manipulators. General admission - 50 and 75 cents. Brown Hall, Monday night. An evening of laughter and fun. – The Congo Co. Does not carry any moving picture machine. They don't need one. (NP1)

May 26, 1905 – The show put on by the Congo Comedy Company was witnessed by a good house, and, had it not been for the drenching rain during the entire night, it would have been even more liberally patronized. It was well received by the audience, and all who attended expressed themselves as highly pleased with the performance. The Congo Twins did some very clever acrobatic stunts, and their rifle and baton performance was heartily applauded. Altogether it was a high class, clean, moral show, and the flattering press notices given them has, in no sense, been exaggerated. (NP1)

June 9, 1905 – Mac's Specialty Company has held down the billboards at the Garland Theater for several evenings with a very pleasing repertoire of comedy and other laughable stunts, including the art of hypnotism. Prizes are distributed among the spectators, and each entertainment concludes with a dance. Everybody who has been attending the shows say the entertainments are fine and well worth the price of admission. The show performs again Sunday and Monday nights and leaves for Cody, Tuesday. (NP1)

October 7, 1905 – *Otto Johnson, The Great Comedian, at Brown's Hall, Saturday Night. A Bushel of Fun for Fun-Loving People.* The only original Otto Johnson, the great comedian, will give an entertainment tonight at Brown's Hall. Brighter, clever and more funny than ever. Admission - 50 cents and 25 cents. There's a treat in store for you. Come and have a good laugh. (NP1)

October 15, 1915 – The Negro Minstrel Show, on Monday night of last week, was enjoyed by a large house. (NP2)

And there were lectures:

February 16, 1917 – The temperance Lecture delivered here Thursday night was well attended. The lecture was [given by] A.B. Crabbe of Cheyenne, State Superintendent of the Anti-saloon League. (NP2)

June 14, 1918 – Red Fox at Garland – Red Fox, the Indian lecturer who appeared in Powell, Wednesday night, will address the people of Garland on Friday night of this week. To a *Tribune* reporter, Mr. Red Fox spoke very complimentarily of Powell and the lively bunch of people we have here, and he thought that he would like to return to Powell, in the fall, to organize a Tipi Order, a branch whose society, he thought might do well in this community. This is a secret order, somewhat similar to other lodges, but has to do entirely with the great outdoors and the life of the Indian people. (NP2)

If anyone was unable to attend any of the entertainment troupes, lectures, dances, or movies, he still had the opportunity to attend one of the many other social gatherings. Several groups and private individuals hosted parties, fund raisers and holiday parties.

September 8, 1905 – A most delightful housewarming was given by Merchant Long in his elegant new residence out on the homestead. Refreshments were served, and a glorious dance was indulged in until a late hour, and all who attended pronounced the affair a huge success. (NP1)

December 2, 1905 – *The Guard* force, those that were at home, are greatly indebted to "Aunt" Mary Hopkin of the Garland Hotel, for the best, most tasty, and delicious Thanksgiving dinner it has ever been our good fortune to sit up to. It was well cooked, there was plenty for all, and a large number sat down to dinner; everyone said it was a splendid feast. Aunt Mary has just secured the services of a professional cook, and to say that he is a Jim Dandy is none too much said. Had our wife and the other members of *The Guard* staff been with us, we should have enjoyed it even more, if that were possible. (NP1)

July 7, 1906 – Party at Hurst's. A delightful social evening occurred Wednesday, July 4th, at the residence of A.A. Hurst and family. All Garland citizens, who had not gone to other towns to celebrate, were invited to participate in the event, which was given with the true spirit of sociability which characterizes Garland.

The company was entertained until supper at 10:00 o'clock with music and games. At 10:00, all present sat down to a delightful repast. After this was completed, dancing was started and splendid music was furnished by Miss McCullock and J.F. Jensen, and the young folks [were] given an opportunity to enjoy themselves until the wee hours of July 5th. (NP1)

In 1917 and 1918, the Dorcas Class of Garland, actively raised money and supported the Red Cross by hosting a moonlight picnic, dinners, cake auctions, rallies, and socials.

January 15, 1915 – The "sock social" given Thursday evening, was a great success in every way. The girls arranged a splendid program and also prepared an excellent lunch. The church was decorated with socks of all shapes, colors, and sizes. Some of the socks were done in beautiful water colors by Adel Harvey. The program was as follows:

Song "Wyoming"	Dorcas Class
Solo, Vocal	Mrs. Gotfriedson
Instrument Solo	Neva Starr
Recitation	Carol Brown
Vocal Duet	Irene and Wanda Lampman
Vocal Solo	Laura Reese
Instrumental Solo	Mrs. A Hancock
Vocal Duet	Leona Sprague, E.D. Richards

After the program, the girls served sandwiches, pickles, and coffee, and everyone went home feeling that they had had a splendid time.

The Dorcas Class wishes to thank all persons who helped them in the "sock social" both in coming and in helping with the program. (NP2)

During the late 20's and 30's, some residents remember going to the movies in Garland. They were offered by a traveling group who projected the picture onto the back of one of the buildings in town, similar to a drive-in movie. Jack VanLake remembered riding the bicycle he got for Christmas down

Garland East End Club. Photo courtesy of Norman "Pete" Woods

to Garland to watch the movies during the summer months. Everyone sat on the ground, and the cost was 10 cents. (126)

Sports activities also brought the community together. Garland did not have a recreation office, like many towns have today, so they organized an athletic club. The most talked about and popular sport was baseball. Garland was very proud of its baseball teams. Almost no one missed a game. Many of the players were pretty good. Pete Woods, Howard Hart, Earl Basham, and Tesla Green are some of the names that come up often when folks talk about the baseball teams. Pete Woods's name is repeated over and over as an impressive baseball player. Howard Hart, Mr. Meyers, and Loren Hiller were pitchers for the men's team, at different times. There was a boy's baseball team, a men's team, and a women's softball team for awhile. Colette Gimmeson remembers that she and two team-mates, Rosie Slack and Bonnie Hiller, played on the softball team. Some of the girls who weren't on the softball team, became cheerleaders for the games. The baseball diamond was located north of the railroad tracks, on the east side of town, behind what is today the Lawrence house. It wasn't a fancy field, but it gave the teams enough area to practice and to play. It was not uncommon to see men running the bases in irrigation boots. The men's games were played on Sunday afternoons and the others were held on week nights. All three teams traveled to different communities to compete - to Powell, Cody, Deaver, Elk Basin, and Willwood. On occasion, the boy's team would challenge the men's team to a game. One such game was reported on by *The Powell Tribune* in April of 1915. *The Tribune* reported that the men's team beat the boy's team 31 to 3, partially due to the fact that the boys just could-

A Starr Club quilt that belonged to Bessie Gimmeson. Bessie used some of her old aprons to quilt her piece.

n't hit as hard as the men could. Like all community sports teams, the teams had to have uniforms, gloves, and balls. They had no sponsors, so they had to have fundraisers. In 1915, the boy's baseball club decided they would perform a play and have a box supper.

March 26, 1915 – The boys of the baseball club are practicing hard on their play to be given the 8th of April. Their tickets will be on sale at the post office from March 23 to 27, inclusive. They have the seats numbered, and if you want a good seat, go early and buy your ticket. Charges are 15 and 25 cents. The cast of characters is as follows: Mr. Pepperpod, an elderly citizen – Hill Campbell, Charley Finch, a gardener – Orley VanEman, Johnny Stockes, a footman – Fleming Kilgore, John Beauchamp, a student – George Cline, Charles Beauchamp, a soldier – Earl Campbell, Mrs. Pepperpod an old maid, subject to fits – Thura Campbell, June and Julia, wards of Mr. Pepperpod – Josie Heaston, Clara Atkins. Besides the play, there are several interesting numbers on the program. Everyone come. (NP2)

It is evident that football and basketball were not as popular as baseball and softball were in the Garland community. Basketball is only mentioned as a sport that the residents remember, and there were only a few who recall anything at all about football. Alden Anderson remembers that when he was in the eighth grade, he had a teacher who was interested in football, so he organized an eighth grade team. They practiced by dividing the team in to two groups who played against each other. Alden only remembers playing one other game, and that was against Powell. He describes the Powell boys as big and says that he felt lucky that the Garland team made at least one touchdown. (I1)

As if school, church, social engagements, and sports didn't keep the community members busy enough, many were involved in men's and women's Clubs. The Garland Men's Club was politically influential. They discussed items related to the school board or county and even tried to influence how the county was managed. For instance, this group was instrumental in getting the rural electrifications system to Garland and starting the Garland Light and Power Company. The Men's Club met in the school building. The Women's Club supplied delicious meals for their meetings. It was a well-known fact that the women in Garland were wonderful cooks, and that drew more men into the meetings, maybe helping to promote their political influence. The Men's Club also sponsored several activities that might boost membership. They headed up fishing trips to Yellowstone, wrestling tournaments, and boxing matches. Darwin Franklin remembered being roped into one of the boxing matches.

"I boxed one time with Jack Lewis. We had a big fight, and they called it a draw, the rascals. We didn't have a ring. We were just in the middle of the club, so the men could see. They had a boundary, I suppose. It was just to fill in time, I think, but Joe Bob Cubbage was the MC, and Boy, did he make it sound big! " (I9)

The Women of Garland also organized a Ladies' Aid Society, The East End Economics Club, and the Starr Club, as well as Women's Club. While these may be different organizations, often their missions were similar - to support the community. The women sponsored bazaars and dinners. The money earned was then used to help families in need, purchase new gas lamps for the church, or anything else the community might need. They prepared meals for families when the wife/mother was ill and helped to gather items for the Red Cross. At their meetings, they would have demonstrations and programs about the newest cooking and canning techniques or aid opportunities. The group would also quilt, making several quilts displaying the names of the members. Each member would make a quilt block with their name on it, and the blocks were then sewed into the quilt. Several of these quilts still exist.

The community members of Garland were never bored, and if they were, it was their own fault. Their everyday farming and ranching activities should have kept them busy enough, but most were also active in one or more of the many community activities. It is said that a family that plays together, stays together. That could be proven in the case of Garland. Not only did the residents become a close knit community by studying, playing, and working together; they became a family.

A copy of the cover of the East End Club record book from 1948. Courtesy of Ted Lord.

Chapter 10 - Matters of Life and Death

It seems only fitting to end a book about a town that is all but gone by discussing its doctors, the health of the community, and, of course its cemetery. Early on, Garland did have its own doctors and cemetery, but like most things, they too, moved to Powell. Many of the residents interviewed barely knew there was a Garland cemetery, but all remembered the doctors they had through the years.

In the beginning, Garland was without a doctor. Early residents relied on home remedies, their own knowledge of first aid, and Divine Providence to keep them well.

October 21, 1905 – Garland has been exceptionally free from sickness this year, thanks to the mercies of an overruling Providence. We hope it will so continue. (NP1)

November 18, 1905 – E.C. Spencer, who is working for the Garland Lumber Company, one day last week, fell very heavily from the top of a high load of lumber, a large pile of it falling upon him before he was able to extricate himself. Luckily for him, he escaped with some minor bruises, and, later in the day, resumed work. (NP1)

January 6, 1906 –Everybody in town is coughing, coughing, coughing. Most everyone has a bad cold. Otherwise, the health of the people is good. The editor's wife was taken ill very suddenly on Thursday, but we are pleased to report her convalescing today. (NP1)

Throughout 1906, *The Garland Guard* enthusiastically reported on several different doctors who considered locating in Garland. Some of them inspected the area, a few did work as they passed through, and while others set up shop, none of the early prospects stayed long. Rumors of a hospital never materialized. It is possible the doctors were drawn to other parts of the Basin, closer to the work being done by the government on the Shoshone Irrigation Project.

February 3, 1906 – *Physicians Coming to Garland* Dr. Earl Wheedon of Denver, Colo., and Dr. E.B. Oliver of Sioux City, Iowa, have formed a partnership of practicing physicians and will locate in Garland in a few days. Both these gentlemen were in the Basin last week and after visiting all the principal towns in the country, concluded that Garland was good enough for them.

It is the intention of these gentlemen to erect a hospital, at this point, where they will be able to properly care for any who may be taken ill or who may be accidentally injured during construction of the big government canal and tunnel at Corbett and east of there.

This is a very excellent idea, as the doctors come here highly recommended and intend location here permanently. We take this means of introducing Doctors Wheedon and Oliver to the people of Big Horn County and bespeak for them the confidence and patronage of the people, wherever the services of a physician are needed, and on behalf of the people of Garland, we extend them a hearty welcome to this young and thriving city. (NP1)

April 7, 1906 – Dr. Cole is doing some good work among the few that are sick among us. He is giving excellent satisfaction. (NP1)

While the hospital never materialized, by 1916, there had been two attempts to set up drug stores. In 1906, Dr. Robbins, who had been doing medical and surgical work in Lovell for the railroad, purchased a lot near the Garland Mercantile and set up a drug store. It is unclear if Dr. Robbins's drug store was at all successful, but, apparently it eventually went out of business. In 1915, Dr. Terwilliger rented the Lee Hotel building and set up a "first class drug store" that was ready for business in October. (NP1) This attempt was also not a long-lasting endeavor. While these were mentioned, most of the residents interviewed remembered going to Powell or getting their medical supplies from the Watkins and Raleigh men.

Dr. Graham, Dr. Mills, and Dr. Whitlock are the doctors most of the residents remember. Dr. Mills and Dr. Graham had offices in Powell, and Dr. Whitlock established and worked in the hospital. Dr. Graham was a very busy man. He was always nice and did what he could to help. He made house calls in his old Plymouth or Buick and was the local pediatrician. With the help of midwives, Mrs. Peterson or Mrs. VanEmmons, he delivered several of the Garland children. After the delivery, the midwives would stay with the family to help with the new baby and to help with chores until the mother had recuperated. Cecilia Hedricks wrote home in 1917, telling her family that Dr. Graham charged $25 to deliver their baby and that they paid Mrs. VanEmmons $22.50 for her week and a half stay. (B5) Both Dr. Mills and Dr. Graham were available for emergencies. When Loretta Meyers was thrown from her horse and hit her head on the cement head gate, Dr. Mills came to sew her up. (I2)

In the days before immunizations, if the doctors weren't attending to deliveries and emergencies, they were trying to contain outbreaks of flu, mumps, measles, small pox, chicken pox, whooping cough, diphtheria, and scarlet fever. In December of 1917, Dr. Mills examined the children at the school for whooping cough. He did not discover any cases, but did advise those with symptoms to stay at home. (NP1) (Quarantines seemed to be the most effective way of managing the spread of this and other illnesses though they did not always work.) In 1918, the Basin experienced a flu epidemic, as did most of the country. Burchell Hopkin remembers his dad telling him that when his uncles got the flu, they rented one of the rooms in the Hopkin Hotel. They didn't want to spread the illness. However, many people got sick, and some died. Robert White reports in the *Frannie-Deaver Proposition* that in 1918, there were 300 cases of flu in Cowley. Ten deaths in Cowley and Lovell were reported due to the flu. (B10)

Many residents remember quarantines as being almost as scary as actually being sick. The doctor would determine the illness and whether the family was contagious. If the doctor determined that they were, the home was quarantined. A sign was posted on the outside of the house. The sign would warn of the quarantine and state the illness that was being contained. "Quarantine, there is flu in this home. Don't come in." (I16) The signs were not only effective in keeping others away; they also worked as a warning system. As soon as one sign was posted, the women of the community went into action, taking all of the necessary precautions to keep the spread of the illness to a minimum. (I14) Jack VanLake remembered going to visit the Franklins and finding out that they were quarantined for mumps.

"Darwin's folks had four or five boys. I remember going down to Franklins to visit, and we couldn't get in. All of the boys were looking out the windows at us, and they all had mumps." (I26)

The length of the quarantines varied. Lloyd Killiam remembers being in quarantine for two weeks for whooping cough and mumps, while Merl Gimmeson remembered being quarantined for six weeks for small pox. On the occasion when a doctor was not available, or a family couldn't afford the doctor, there were home remedies. Fay Smith remembers several remedies from her childhood:

"Goodness yes. I ate enough Watkin's Liniments growing up. Mom gave it to us for everything. We didn't go to the emergency room every time we got a cold. They had all kinds of ideas about what was good for us. I don't know where they got the ideas, maybe just made them up. There weren't any Indians around to tell them. I think Mom gave us kerosene and sugar for the croup, just a teaspoon. They gave us sagebrush tea in the spring. That was pretty wicked stuff. What else did we get? If we had sore throats, she put soda in our throats. She could shoot it down there and get it right down there on your sore throat. Things like that." (I25)

While doctors do all they can, death is a fact of life. Little is known about the Garland Cemetery or about those who are laid to rest there. There are no official documents of Garland's cemetery or the possibility of a cemetery board. The only recorded or written information is from the memories of Warren Cubbage and Les Lawrence.

It is assumed that burials were taking place, beginning as early as 1901. The Garland Cemetery is located northeast of town on A.B. Campbell's homestead. (Campbell was a minister and apparently made a verbal donation of the land for the cemetery.) It has been estimated that 25 to 30 burials took place in the cemetery. Most were marked with wooden crosses, and some with headstones. (MSL 3) Warren Cubbage remembered, in his younger days, seeing the wooden crosses and the fence that surrounded the cemetery. Warren wasn't sure when, but at some point, the fence was knocked down, and the livestock began to graze the area. The cattle knocked down the wooden crosses and no one noticed. By this time, the kin of the deceased had left the area. Eventually, all of the crosses rotted, leaving behind only the headstones. (I6)

A map of the Garland cemetery, drawn by Les Lawrence to Ms. Sharon Lass Field.

One of the headstones that remains today belongs to George Shoemaker. Walt Preis' told Theodore Shoemaker's experience of his father's death in his article, "The Innkeeper's Grave at Garland."

"Theodore was working at a mine in Leadville, Colorado. He received word that his father had died. His father and stepmother, at the time, ran a hotel in Garland, Wyoming. It was the middle of the winter and cold. He asked to get leave from his job. He must get to Garland and see to his father's burial. But mostly he must find out the cause of his father's death. (None of the family had much trust in the stepmother.)

Well – When he got to Garland – the body was still lying, frozen solid, in a storeroom in the hotel. He was told his father had died of pneumonia. He needed to get [back] to his job in Colorado, so he made arrangements, with someone else, to see to the burial and returned to Colorado." (MSA&P 8)

The following is George Shoemaker's obituary that was printed in *The Garland Guard.*

December 23, 1905 – Obituary. George Shoemaker was born December 18, 1848, and had he lived eight days more, would have been 57 years of age. The place of his birth was Perry Co., Indiana. He died at his home in Garland, Wyoming, on December 10, 1905. In 1880, he moved to Smith Co., Kansas where he lived until 1890, at which time he moved to Franklin Co., Nebraska. In 1904, he moved into Wyoming, settling at Germania in Big Horn County, and, in the fall of the present year, came to Garland and took charge of the Gate City Hotel, which he acquired by purchase. He was conducting his business when death cut him short. He was married in 1869 to Emeline Tylor.

Mr. Shoemaker was again married in 1894 to Sarah A. Bullock, who with son, Adam C., born to them, remains to mourn the loss of a dutiful husband and loving father.

Mr. Shoemaker was a whole souled, honest hearted man, kind and generous almost to a fault, and he leaves behind many friends in various parts of the country. The sorrowing widow and children have the sympathy of the entire community.

The funeral services were held at the late residence of the deceased on Thursday afternoon, December 14th, and were conducted by the Rev. W.O. Harper of Cody, in the presence of relatives and many friends of the departed, and the body was consigned to his last resting place in the Garland Cemetery.

Mr. Shoemaker was a typical westerner, a throrough farmer, and had a great faith in the future of the Big Horn Basin. He was heavily interested in numerous enterprises. His health was vigorous, and his sudden death came as a great surprise to his many friends. May he rest in peace. (NP1)

Ralph Elmo's headstone in the Garland Cemetery. 2003

George Shoemaker's headstone in the Garland Cemetery. 2003

After years of neglect and vandalism the cemetery is hardly discernible today. If you look closely, near George Shoemaker's headstone which is surrounded by an iron fence, you will find Cove Harmon's and Ralph Elmo Harmon's headstones. Cove Harmon's headstone reads – Born 5 Jan. 1877, Died 15 Nov, 1915, "Gone but not forgotten." Ralph Elmo Harmon's headstone reads – Born 1 Apr, 1913, Died 20 Oct 1915, "Son of Mr. and Mrs. G. Harmon. Gone but not forgotten." Other unmarked graves that are said to remain in the Garland Cemetery are Marie Katherine Malliot - Born 21 April, 1848, Died 23 April, 1909; The Garland railroad section foreman, Carlson; Auston Harrison Campbell – "Died 1920 at age 2 years;" "Angello Monti, worked for the Burlington Railroad, froze to death" – Died 24 March, 1906; Unknown, "a railroad hitchhiker killed by Sheriff Loomis," and one last Unknown, "killed by a shooting at a nearby Garland stock corral." (MSL3) The legend behind the shooting at the Garland stock corral is the kind old Westerns are made of. A stranger walked up to a cowboy standing at the corrals and asked if Garland had a cemetery yet. The cowboy replied that Garland did not yet have a cemetery. The stranger replied that he would help them get one established - and shot the cowboy. As the story goes, the cemetery was established, and the cowboy was the first interred.

The remains of the Garland Cemetery. 2003.

Vern Fales tells the story of the hitchhiker killed by Sheriff Loomis.

"One hobo came into town, and the sheriff thought he was a wanted man, but he wasn't sure. So he yelled at the guy, and he wouldn't stop, just kept walking. The sheriff took his pistol and laid it up on his saddle horn, rode up to the guy, identified him, and shot him. And he's buried up there in the cemetery." (I8)

After 1920, the Garland Cemetery became defunct. After that, all deceased residents of Garland, were buried in Powell's Crown Hill Cemetery, and some of those who had been buried in the Garland Cemetery were re-interred there.

Like the headstones in the cemetery, the Church of Garland, the ASI Bean Mill, and a few houses are the only monuments left to remind us of the grand visions of a small town and a community with a lot of heart.

Any effort, such as this one, to preserve the history and the stories about "real" people who settled an area and passed on their heritage, is intended to honor them and pay tribute to their fortitude and spirit. It is also meant to encourage others to carry on worthwhile traditions and to recognize how very important they are.

Sources

Interviews (I#)

Anderson, Alden, November 13, 2003, by Christy Fleming

Brown, Katie, December 9, 2003, by Christy Fleming and Geri Bulkeley

Christiansen, Everett and Martha, April 24, 2002, by Christy Fleming

Cozzens, Lucy, March 31, 2004, by Christy Fleming

Crane, Lucille, Fall 2001, by Christy Fleming

Cubbage, Warren and Johanna, Fall 2001, by Christy Fleming

Fales, Merl, April 1, 2004, by Christy Fleming

Fales, Vern, April 26, 2005, by Christy Fleming

Franklin, Darwin and Nada, November 17, 2003, by Christy Fleming

Gimmeson, Gene, September 15, 2001, and other informal discussions at later dates,
    by Christy Fleming

Gimmeson, Merl and Colette, August 10, 2001, by Christy Fleming

Hart, Hubert and Wanda, November 17, 2003, by Christy Fleming

Hart, Jim and Ruth, October 22, 2001, by Christy Fleming

Heimer, Ethel, October 14, 2003, by Christy Fleming

Hiller, Bonnie, April 23, 2002, by Christy Fleming

Hopkin, Burchell, October 22, 2001, by Christy Fleming

Jones, Earl, October 15, 2004, by Christy Fleming

Jones, Herb and Martha, November 14, 2003, by Christy Fleming

Killiam, Lloyd, May 13, 2002, by Christy Fleming

Lang, Fred, October 13, 2003, by Christy Fleming

Lawrence, Les, October 24, 2001, by Christy Fleming

Lord, Ted and Leona, April 9, 2004, by Christy Fleming

Ries, Joe and Amilia, November 13, 2003, by Christy Fleming

Scott, Melvin and Mary, December 8, 2003, by Christy Fleming

Smith, Fay, November 17, 2003, by Christy Fleming

VanLake, Jack and Shirley, October 13, 2004, by Christy Fleming

Wood, Norman "Pete", October, 24, 2001, By Christy Fleming

Yonts, Irma, several phone conversations and a visit. No formal interview.
    She sent photos, a scrapbook, and information for use in the book.

Books (B#)

Black, Rosa Vida Bischoff., *Lovell, Our Pioneer Heritage*, Olympus Publishing Company, Salt Lake City, Utah, 1984.

Bonner, Robert., *Farm Town, Stories of the Early History of Powell.*, 1999.

Davis, Jonathan and Melba, *They Called it Germania!, The History of Wyoming's Emblem Bench 1893-1939*. Gateway Press, Inc., Baltimore, MD. 2004.

Davis, J. Tom, *Glimpses of Greybull's Past, A History of a Wyoming Railroad Town From 1887 to 1939*. Basin Republican Rustler Printing, Basin, Wyoming 1987.

Hendricks, Cecilia Hennel., *Letters From Honeyhill, A Woman's View of Homesteading ,1914-1922.*, Pruett Publishing Company, Boulder, Colorado, 1990.

Larson, T.A., *History of Wyoming. Second Edition, Revised.*, University of Nebraska Press, Lincoln and London, 1978.

Partridge, Mark N., *With Book and Plow, Revised Edition.*, Family History Publishers, inc., Bountiful, UT., 2003.

Trails and Tales South of the Yellowstone, Trails and Tales. Historical Committee, Midland Printing and Supply Co., Billings, Montana, 1983.

Wasden, David J., *From Beaver to Oil, a Century in the Development of Wyoming's Big Horn Basin.*, Pioneer Printing and Stationery Co., Cheyenne, Wyoming, 1973.

White, Robert, *The Frannie-Deaver Proposition, A Chronicle of Optimism and Alkali.*, Frontier Printing Company, Cheyenne, Wyoming, 1990.

White, Robert, *The Sage Creek Water Wars, Fought with Law Instead of Guns.*, Frontier Printing Company, Cheyenne, Wyoming, 1990.

Woods, Lawrence M., *Wyoming's Bighorn Basin to 1901, A Late Frontier.*, The Arthur H. Clark Company, Spokane, WA., 1997.

Newspapers (NP#)

The Garland Guard – May 5, 1905 through July 7, 1906. Found at the Pioneer Museum in Cowely, Wyoming.

The Powell Tribune – January 1, 1915 through June 14, 1918.

Newspaper Articles (NA#)

"Another Chapter of Area History Ends with Garland Post Office" *Powell Tribune*, Tuesday, March 27, 1973. – Irma Younts Collection.

"Bureau's Ruling Created New City" By Rodger Clawson, Chief Staff Writer. *Billings Gazette.* – Irma Yonts Collection.

"Coal Mine Hill Shows Evidence of Coal Mining in Garland Area" *Powell Tribune*, Thursday, July 1, 1976.

"Garland Church Pays Off its Mortgage" *Powell Tribune*, Thursday, February 21, 1985.

"Garland Home Since 1909" *Powell Tribune*, Date Missing.

"Garland Sleeps at the Crossroads After the Boom of Early-day Growth" *Powell Tribune,* June 14-21, 1959.

"Garland Wyo., Boom Town and Trading Post" *Powell Tribune*, June 14, 1959.

"Garland was Bustling in its Heyday, Development of Powell was a Move Away from the Bright Lights" *Powell Tribune*, Homesteader Days, Thursday, July 25, 1991. – Irma Yonts Collection.

Lovell Chronicle, People, Family Living Today, Anna Parks, No Date or Title.

"History of Garland Presented" *Powell Tribune*, Tuesday, April 28, 1998.

"85,000 Farmers Owned Automobiles in 1910" *Looking at Agriculture Special Edition*, page 5, Tuesday, May 29, 1984.

Miscellaneous Sources

Letters (MSL#)

Letter to Ms. Sharon Lass Field, about the Cemetery, from Les Lawrence.

Letter from A.C. Shoemaker to Mr. Wasden, December 31, 1974.

Articles and Paper (MSA&P #)

Breitweiser, Wayne R., "Down Wind and Across the Coulee."

Hicks, L.N., "History of Park County", Page 61 – 63.

House, Blanche, Report on Early Garland, Wyoming.

Lawrence, Leslie E. and Mildred, Garland, Wyoming "Houses with a Past, This Wyoming Centennial Year" 1988-1989

Pond, Robert A., "Why Does a Town Die?"

Preis, Walt, "The Innkeeper's Grave at Garland."

Wasden, David J., Garland, The Gate City, Cody, Wyoming, March 1980.

Weaver, Paul, A History of Frannie. 1975.

"Garland, The Gate City", page 282-285, unknown source.

"Garland, Wyoming", Taken from Park County Book. Irma Yonts Collection.

Reports (MSR #)

"Corporate History of the Chicago, Burlington, and Quincy Railroad Company and Affiliated Companies" (As of date June 30, 1917), Prepared by W.W. Baldwin, Vice-President.

East End Club Book, 1948, Ted Lord's mother's copy.

Family Histories (MSFH #)

Family History written by Dorothy Wood.

Family History written by Burchel E. Hopkin, 1987. The Hopkin Women's Hotels

Obituaries (MSO #)

Obituary from the *Garland Guard*, December 23, 1905.

Printed in the United States
107631LV00005BA/13-26/P

9 780977 128648